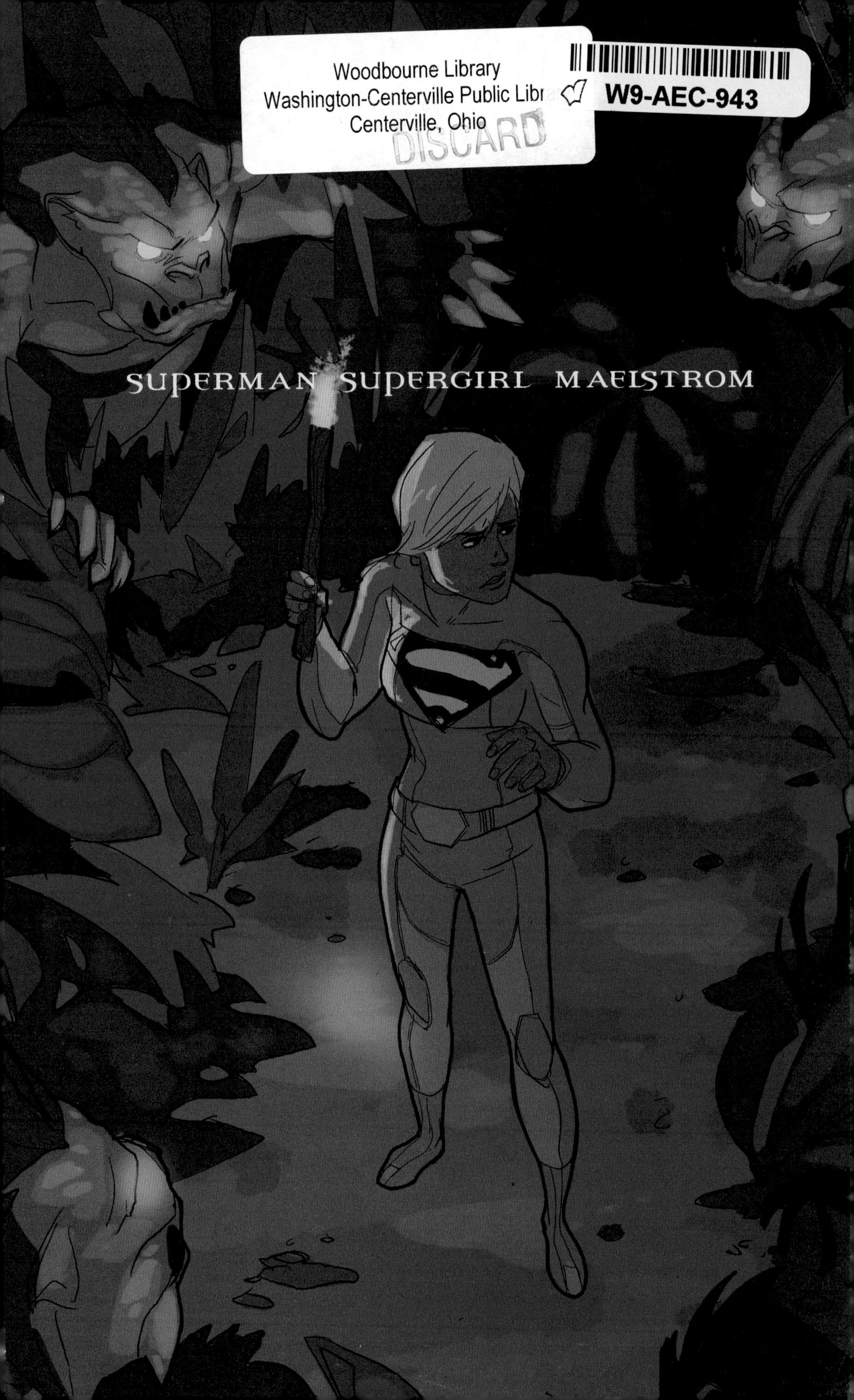
SUPERMAN SUPERGIRL MAELSTROM

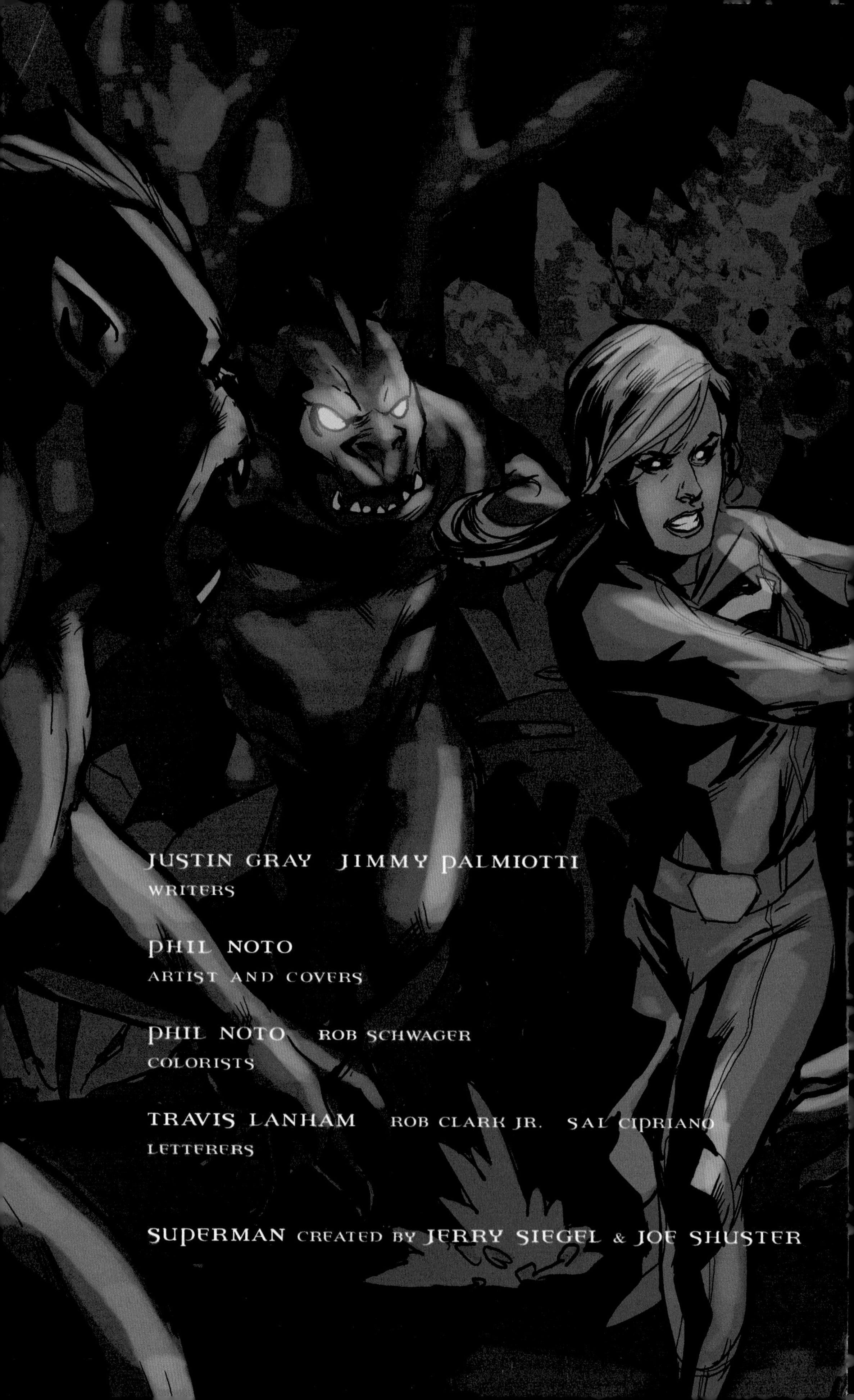

JUSTIN GRAY JIMMY PALMIOTTI
WRITERS

PHIL NOTO
ARTIST AND COVERS

PHIL NOTO ROB SCHWAGER
COLORISTS

TRAVIS LANHAM ROB CLARK JR. SAL CIPRIANO
LETTERERS

SUPERMAN CREATED BY JERRY SIEGEL & JOE SHUSTER

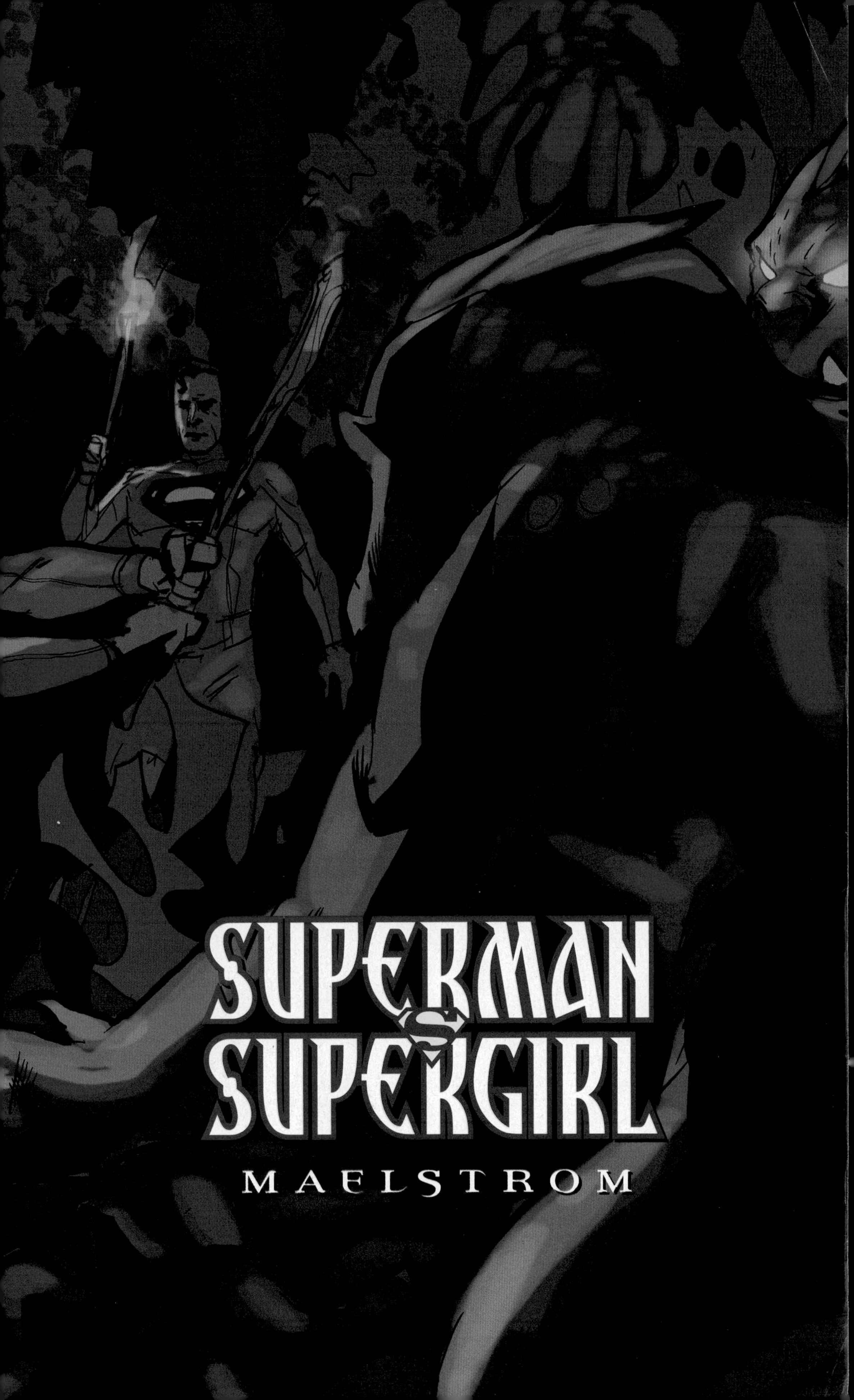
SUPERMAN
SUPERGIRL
MAELSTROM

Dan DiDio   SVP-Executive Editor
Michael Siglain   Editor-original series
Harvey Richards   Assist. Editor-original series
Georg Brewer   VP-Design & DC Direct Creative
Bob Harras   Group Editor-Collected Editions
Peter Hamboussi   Editor
Robbin Brosterman   Design Director-Books

DC COMICS

Paul Levitz   President & Publisher
Richard Bruning   SVP-Creative Director
Patrick Caldon   EVP-Finance & Operations
Amy Genkins   SVP-Business & Legal Affairs
Jim Lee   Editorial Director-WildStorm
Gregory Noveck   SVP-Creative Affairs
Steve Rotterdam   SVP-Sales & Marketing
Cheryl Rubin   SVP-Brand Management

Cover by Phil Noto

DC Comics, 1700 Broadway, New York, NY 10019
A Warner Bros. Entertainment Company
Printed by World Color Press, Inc,
St-Romuald, QC, Canada 11/04/09
First Printing. ISBN: 978-1-4012-2508-7

SUSTAINABLE
FORESTRY
INITIATIVE

Certified Fiber
Sourcing
www.sfiprogram.org

Fiber used in this product line meets the sourcing requirements
of the SFI program. www.sfiprogram.org PWC-SFICOC-260

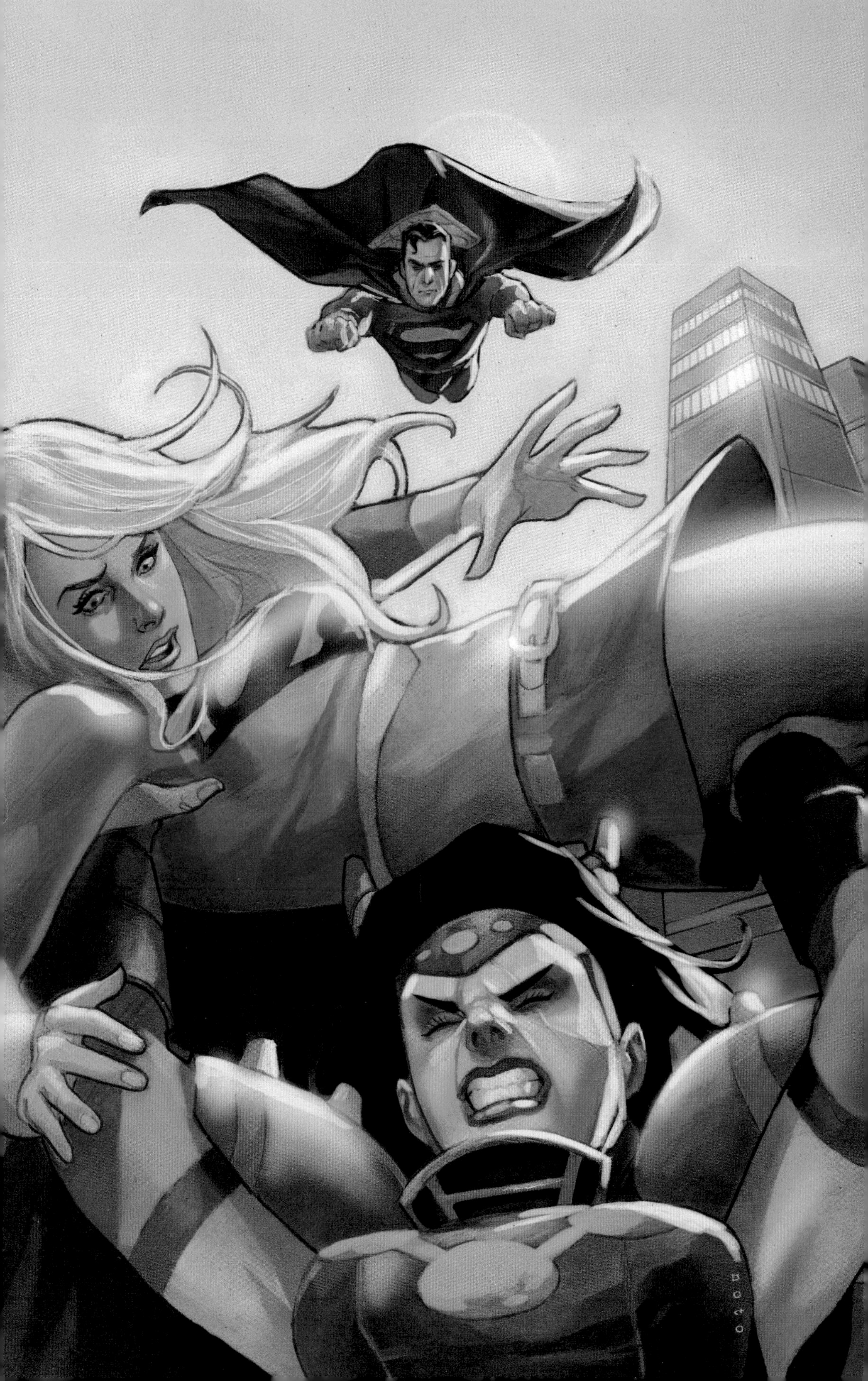

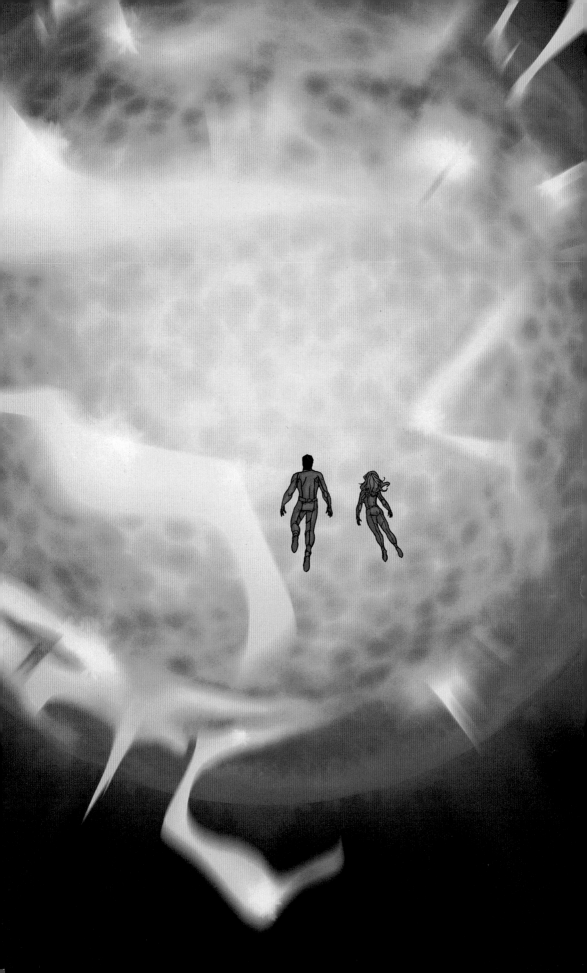

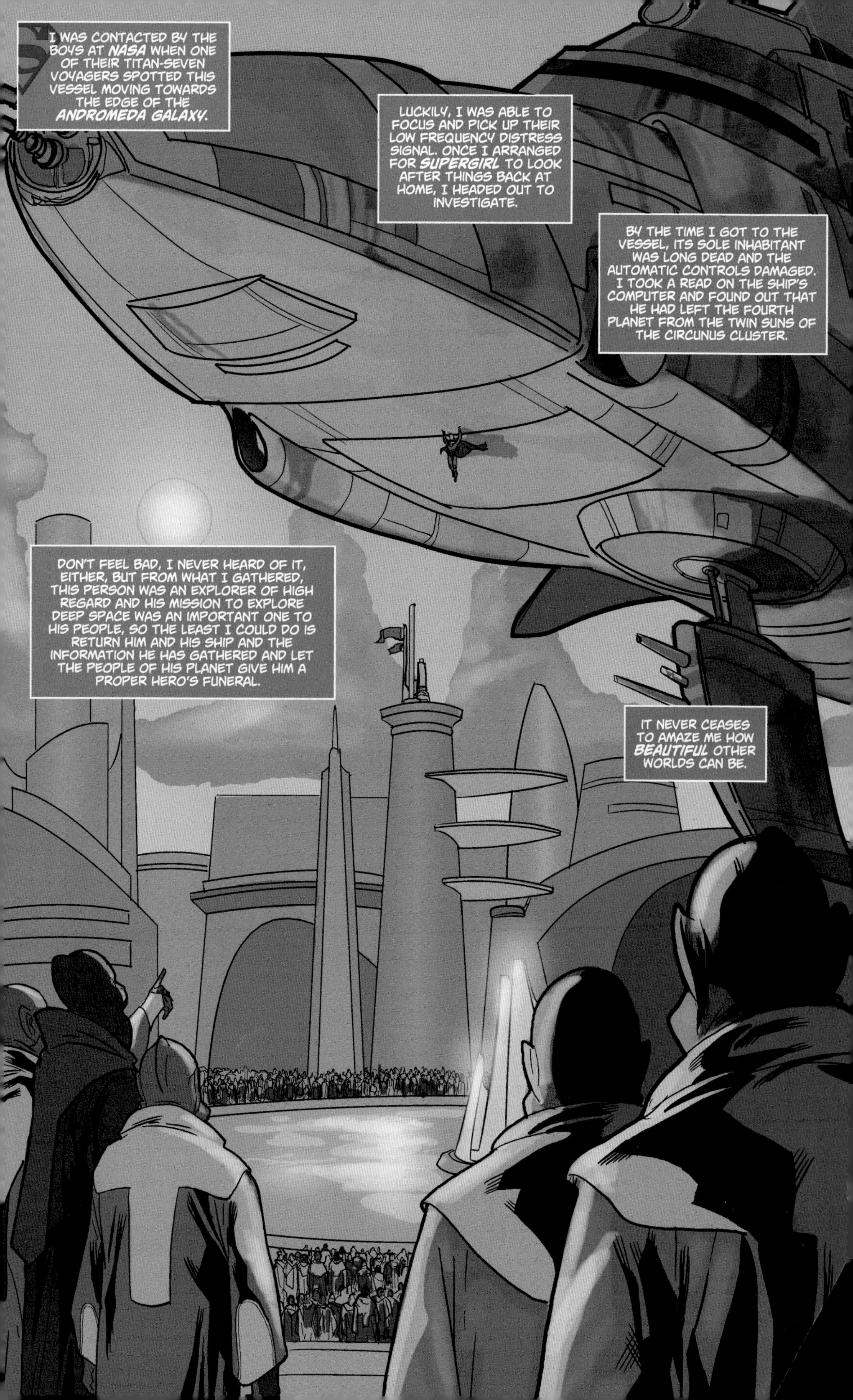
I WAS CONTACTED BY THE BOYS AT NASA WHEN ONE OF THEIR TITAN-SEVEN VOYAGERS SPOTTED THIS VESSEL MOVING TOWARDS THE EDGE OF THE ANDROMEDA GALAXY.
LUCKILY, I WAS ABLE TO FOCUS AND PICK UP THEIR LOW FREQUENCY DISTRESS SIGNAL. ONCE I ARRANGED FOR SUPERGIRL TO LOOK AFTER THINGS BACK AT HOME, I HEADED OUT TO INVESTIGATE.
BY THE TIME I GOT TO THE VESSEL, ITS SOLE INHABITANT WAS LONG DEAD AND THE AUTOMATIC CONTROLS DAMAGED. I TOOK A READ ON THE SHIP'S COMPUTER AND FOUND OUT THAT HE HAD LEFT THE FOURTH PLANET FROM THE TWIN SUNS OF THE CIRCUNUS CLUSTER.
DON'T FEEL BAD, I NEVER HEARD OF IT, EITHER, BUT FROM WHAT I GATHERED, THIS PERSON WAS AN EXPLORER OF HIGH REGARD AND HIS MISSION TO EXPLORE DEEP SPACE WAS AN IMPORTANT ONE TO HIS PEOPLE, SO THE LEAST I COULD DO IS RETURN HIM AND HIS SHIP AND THE INFORMATION HE HAS GATHERED AND LET THE PEOPLE OF HIS PLANET GIVE HIM A PROPER HERO'S FUNERAL.
IT NEVER CEASES TO AMAZE ME HOW BEAUTIFUL OTHER WORLDS CAN BE.

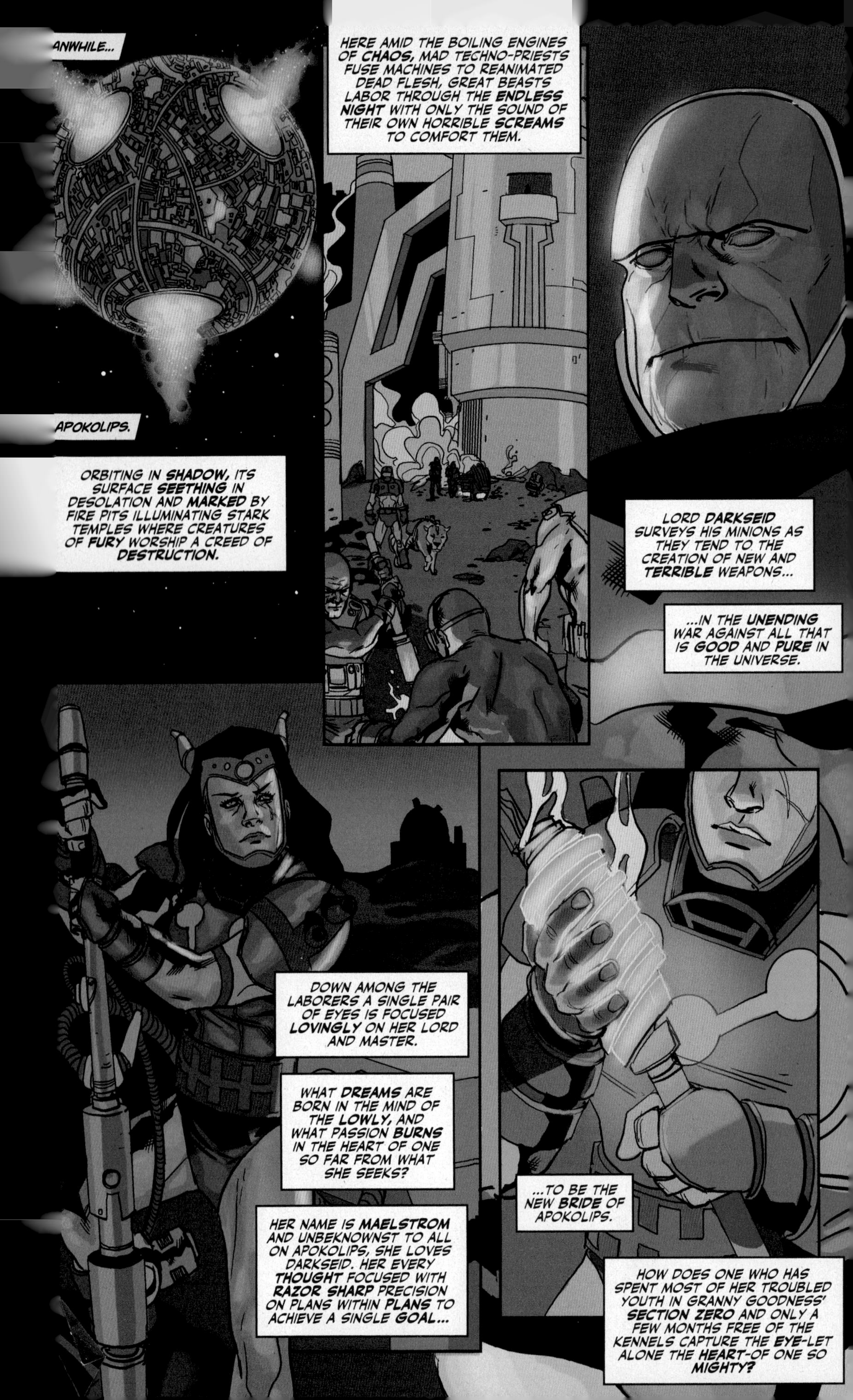
ANWHILE...
APOKOLIPS.
ORBITING IN SHADOW, ITS SURFACE SEETHING IN DESOLATION AND MARKED BY FIRE PITS ILLUMINATING STARK TEMPLES WHERE CREATURES OF FURY WORSHIP A CREED OF DESTRUCTION.
HERE AMID THE BOILING ENGINES OF CHAOS, MAD TECHNO-PRIESTS FUSE MACHINES TO REANIMATED DEAD FLESH, GREAT BEASTS LABOR THROUGH THE ENDLESS NIGHT WITH ONLY THE SOUND OF THEIR OWN HORRIBLE SCREAMS TO COMFORT THEM.
LORD DARKSEID SURVEYS HIS MINIONS AS THEY TEND TO THE CREATION OF NEW AND TERRIBLE WEAPONS...
...IN THE UNENDING WAR AGAINST ALL THAT IS GOOD AND PURE IN THE UNIVERSE.
DOWN AMONG THE LABORERS A SINGLE PAIR OF EYES IS FOCUSED LOVINGLY ON HER LORD AND MASTER.
WHAT DREAMS ARE BORN IN THE MIND OF THE LOWLY, AND WHAT PASSION BURNS IN THE HEART OF ONE SO FAR FROM WHAT SHE SEEKS?
HER NAME IS MAELSTROM AND UNBEKNOWNST TO ALL ON APOKOLIPS, SHE LOVES DARKSEID. HER EVERY THOUGHT FOCUSED WITH RAZOR SHARP PRECISION ON PLANS WITHIN PLANS TO ACHIEVE A SINGLE GOAL...
...TO BE THE NEW BRIDE OF APOKOLIPS.
HOW DOES ONE WHO HAS SPENT MOST OF HER TROUBLED YOUTH IN GRANNY GOODNESS' SECTION ZERO AND ONLY A FEW MONTHS FREE OF THE KENNELS CAPTURE THE EYE-LET ALONE THE HEART-OF ONE SO MIGHTY?

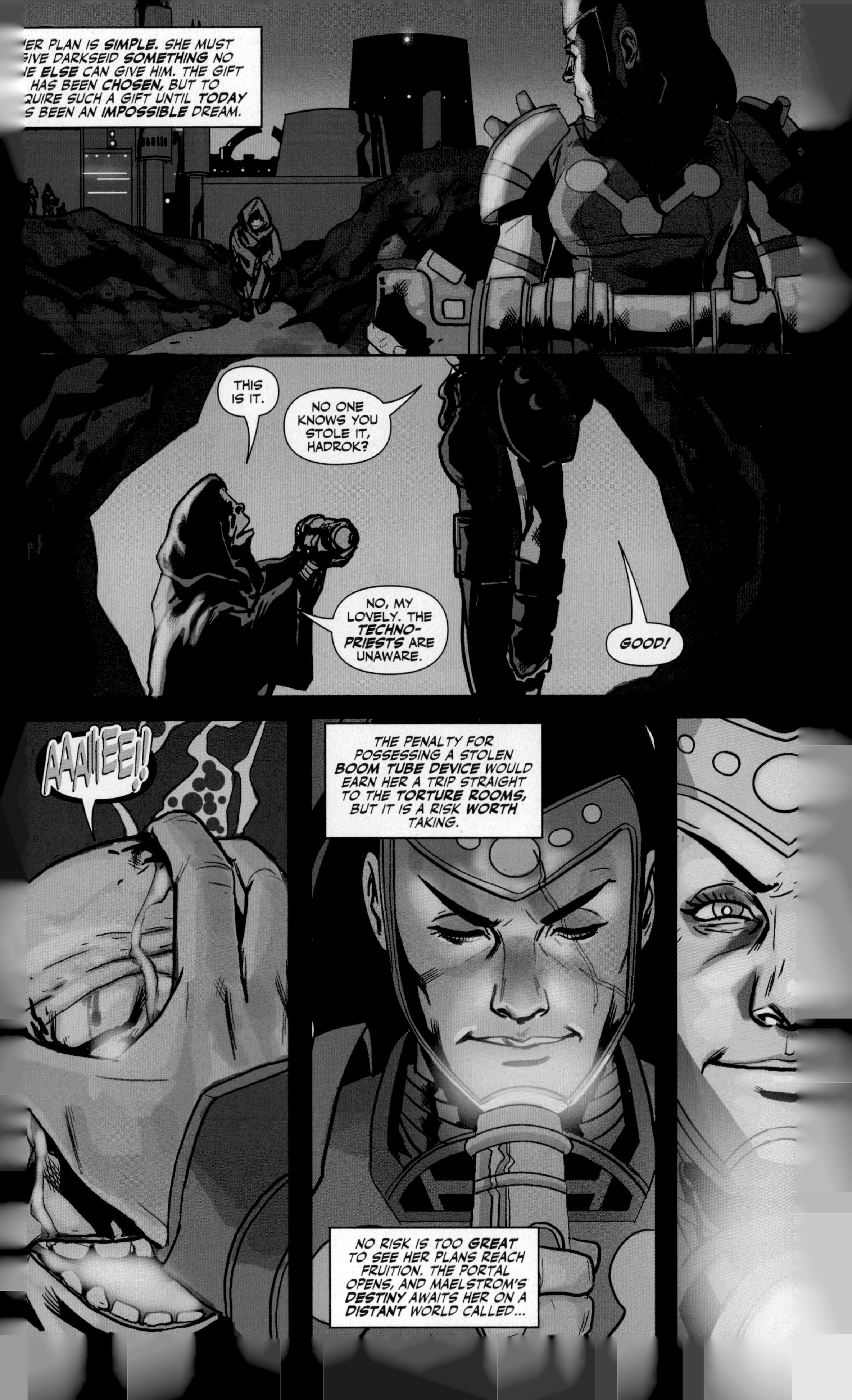
ER PLAN IS **SIMPLE.** SHE MUST GIVE DARKSEID **SOMETHING** NO E **ELSE** CAN GIVE HIM. THE GIFT HAS BEEN **CHOSEN,** BUT TO QUIRE SUCH A GIFT UNTIL **TODAY** S BEEN AN **IMPOSSIBLE** DREAM.
THIS IS IT.
NO ONE KNOWS YOU STOLE IT, HADROK?
NO, MY LOVELY. THE ***TECHNO-PRIESTS*** ARE UNAWARE.
GOOD!
AAAIIEE!!
THE PENALTY FOR POSSESSING A STOLEN **BOOM TUBE DEVICE** WOULD EARN HER A TRIP STRAIGHT TO THE **TORTURE ROOMS,** BUT IT IS A RISK **WORTH** TAKING.
NO RISK IS TOO **GREAT** TO SEE HER PLANS REACH FRUITION. THE PORTAL OPENS, AND MAELSTROM'S **DESTINY** AWAITS HER ON A **DISTANT** WORLD CALLED...

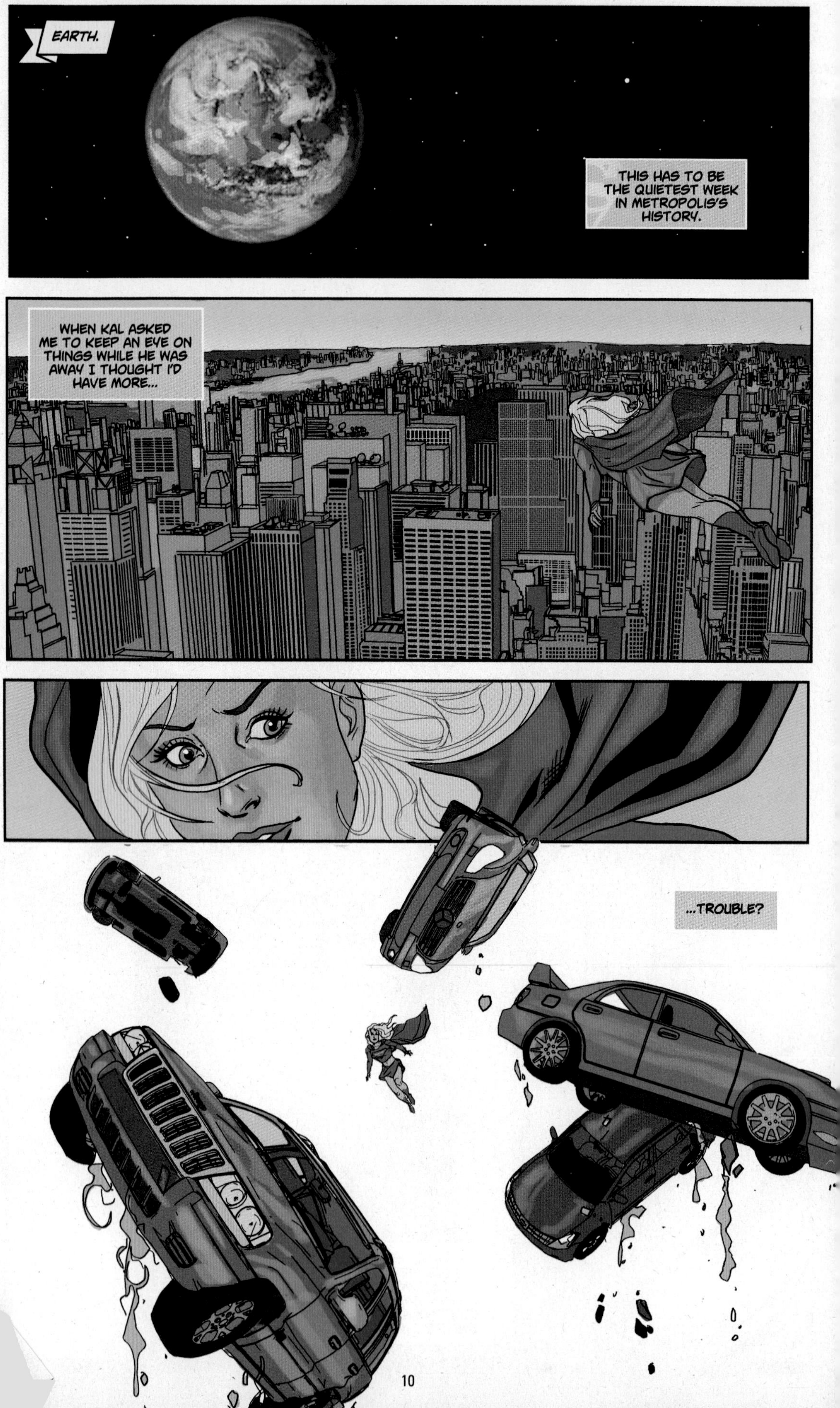
EARTH.
THIS HAS TO BE THE QUIETEST WEEK IN METROPOLIS'S HISTORY.
WHEN KAL ASKED ME TO KEEP AN EYE ON THINGS WHILE HE WAS AWAY I THOUGHT I'D HAVE MORE...
...TROUBLE?

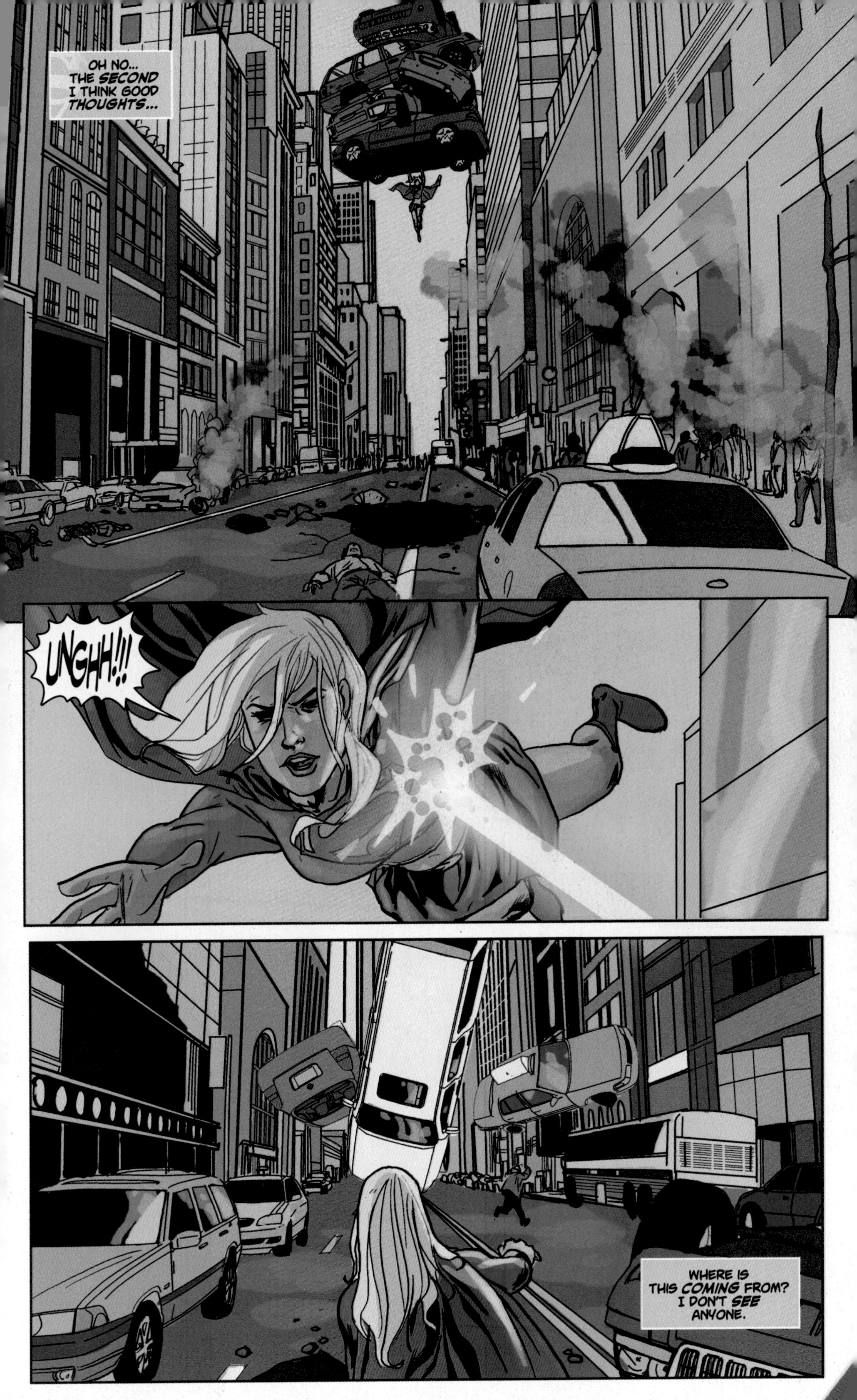
OH NO... THE SECOND I THINK GOOD THOUGHTS...
UNGHH!!!
WHERE IS THIS COMING FROM? I DON'T SEE ANYONE.

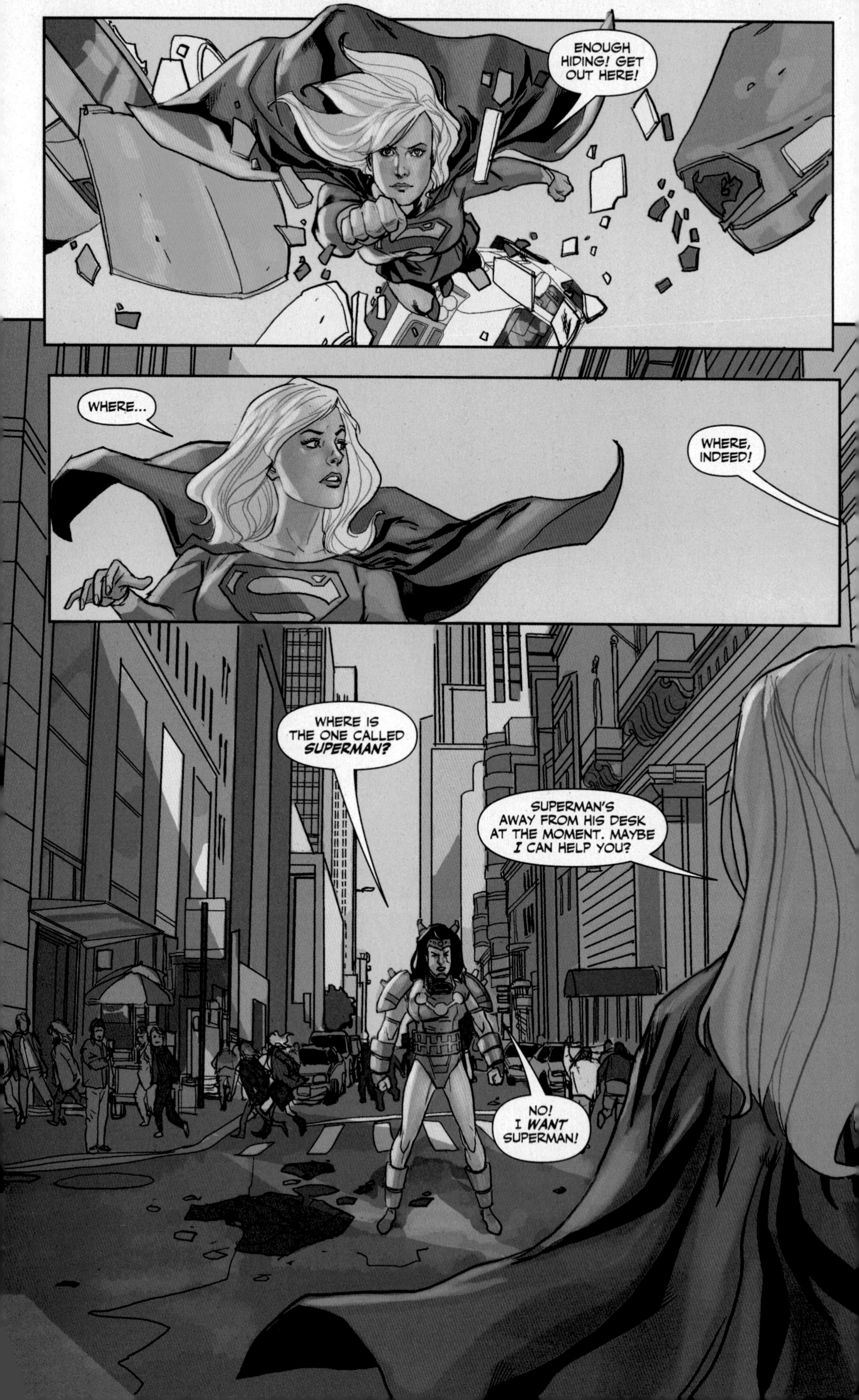

ENOUGH HIDING! GET OUT HERE!
WHERE...
WHERE, INDEED!
WHERE IS THE ONE CALLED *SUPERMAN?*
SUPERMAN'S AWAY FROM HIS DESK AT THE MOMENT. MAYBE *I* CAN HELP YOU?
NO! I *WANT* SUPERMAN!

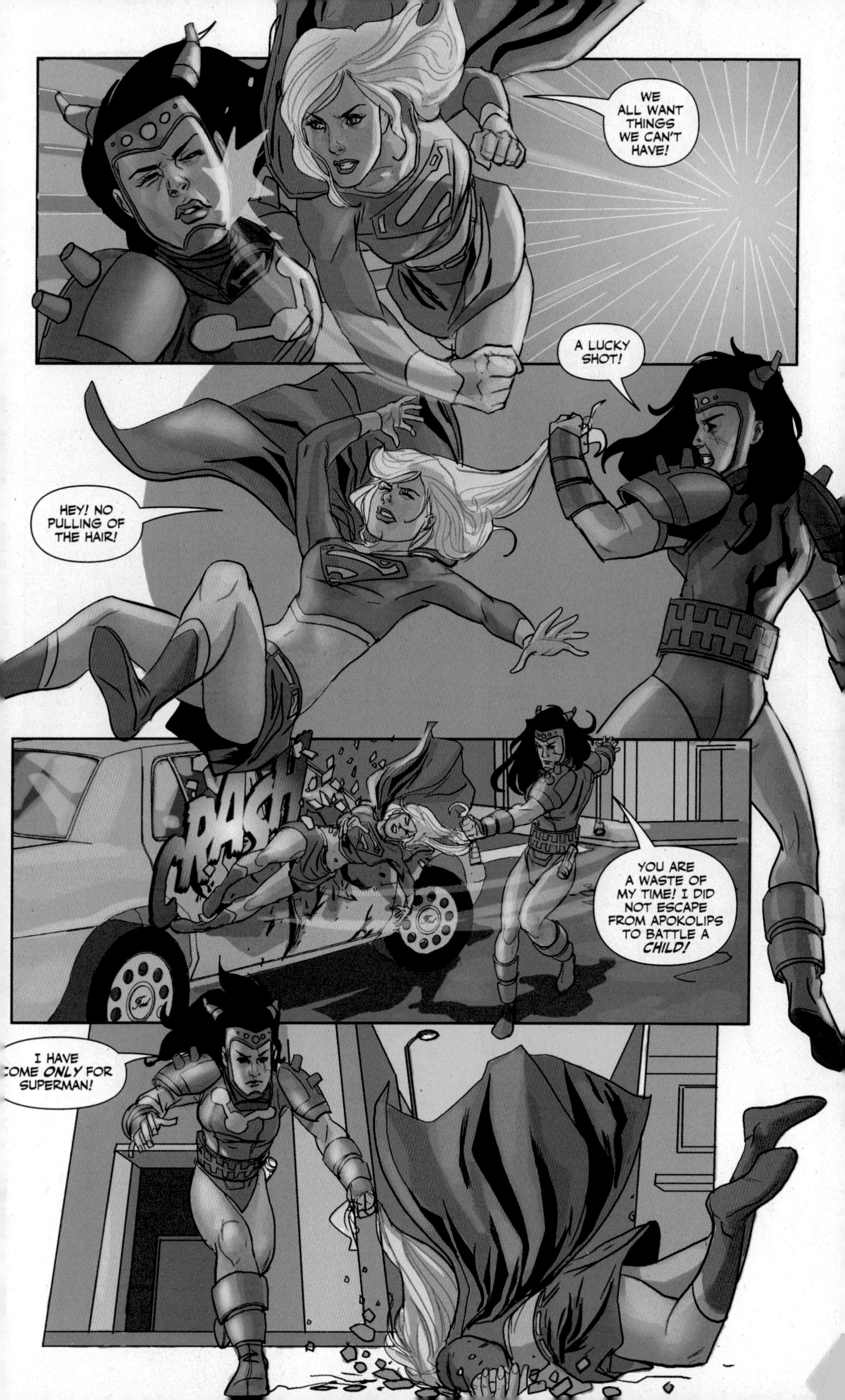
WE ALL WANT THINGS WE CAN'T HAVE!
A LUCKY SHOT!
HEY! NO PULLING OF THE HAIR!
CRASH
YOU ARE A WASTE OF MY TIME! I DID NOT ESCAPE FROM APOKOLIPS TO BATTLE A CHILD!
I HAVE COME ONLY FOR SUPERMAN!

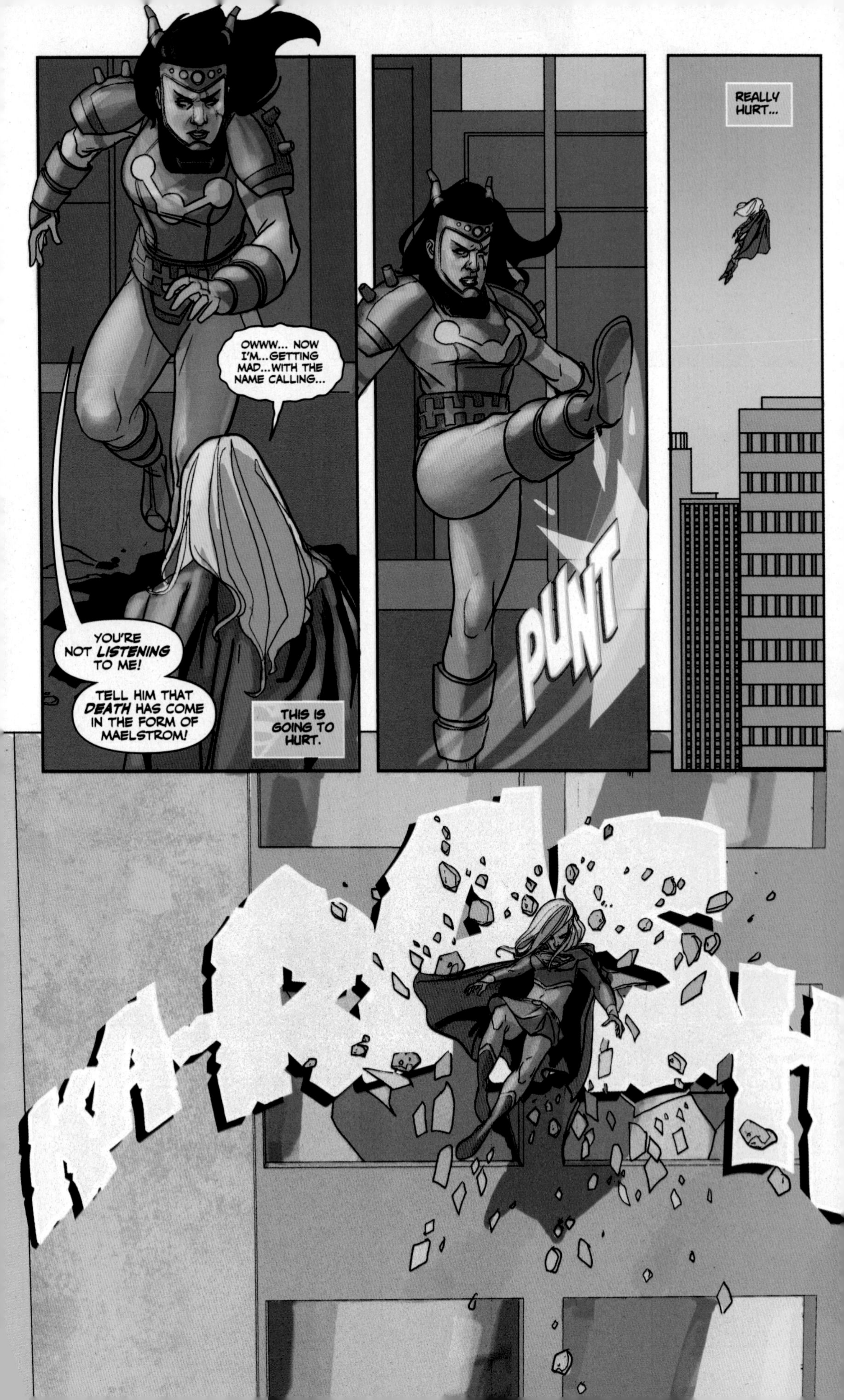
OWWW... NOW I'M...GETTING MAD...WITH THE NAME CALLING...
YOU'RE NOT LISTENING TO ME!
TELL HIM THAT DEATH HAS COME IN THE FORM OF MAELSTROM!
THIS IS GOING TO HURT.
PUNT
REALLY HURT...
KA-BOOSH

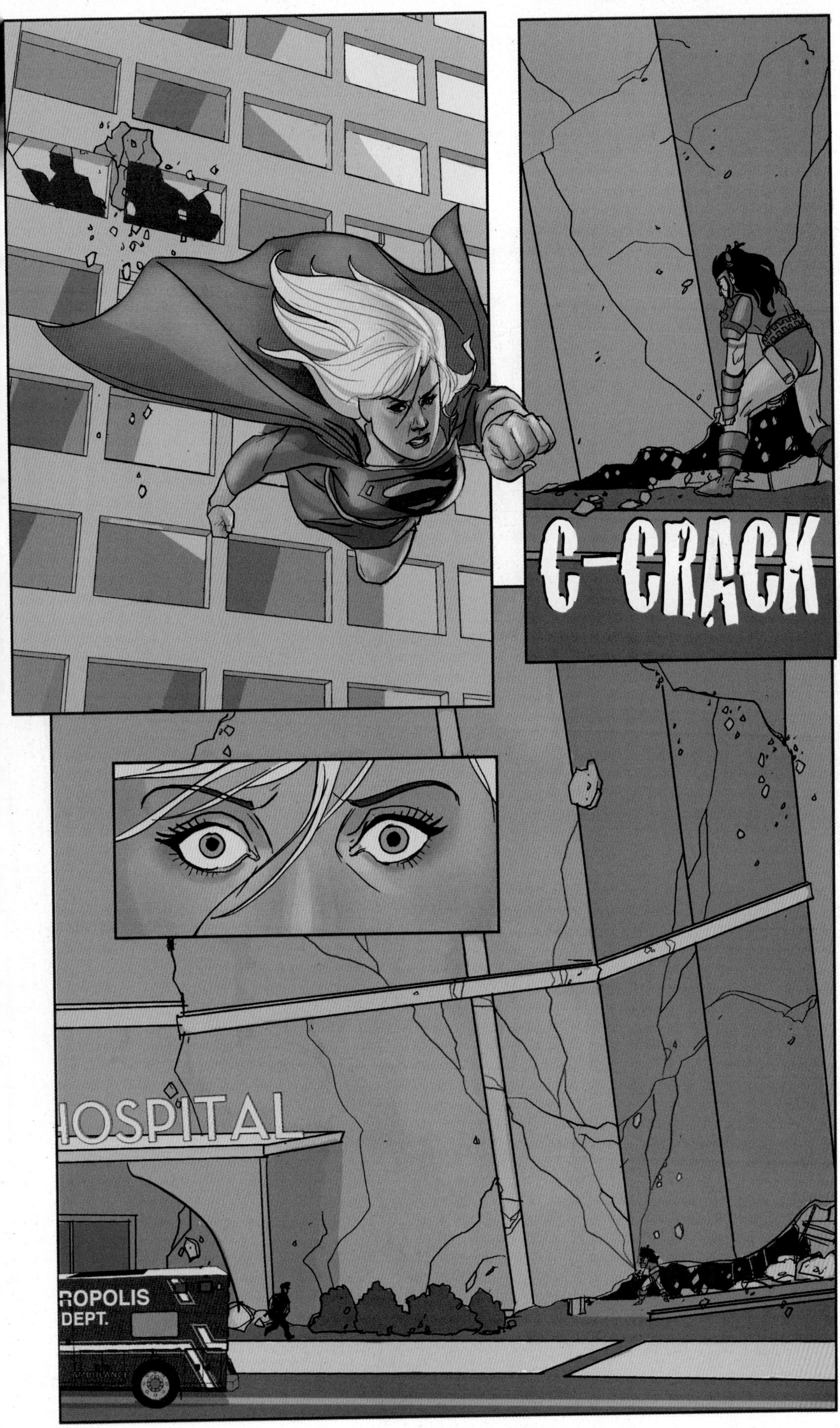
C-CRACK
HOSPITAL
ROPOLIS
DEPT.

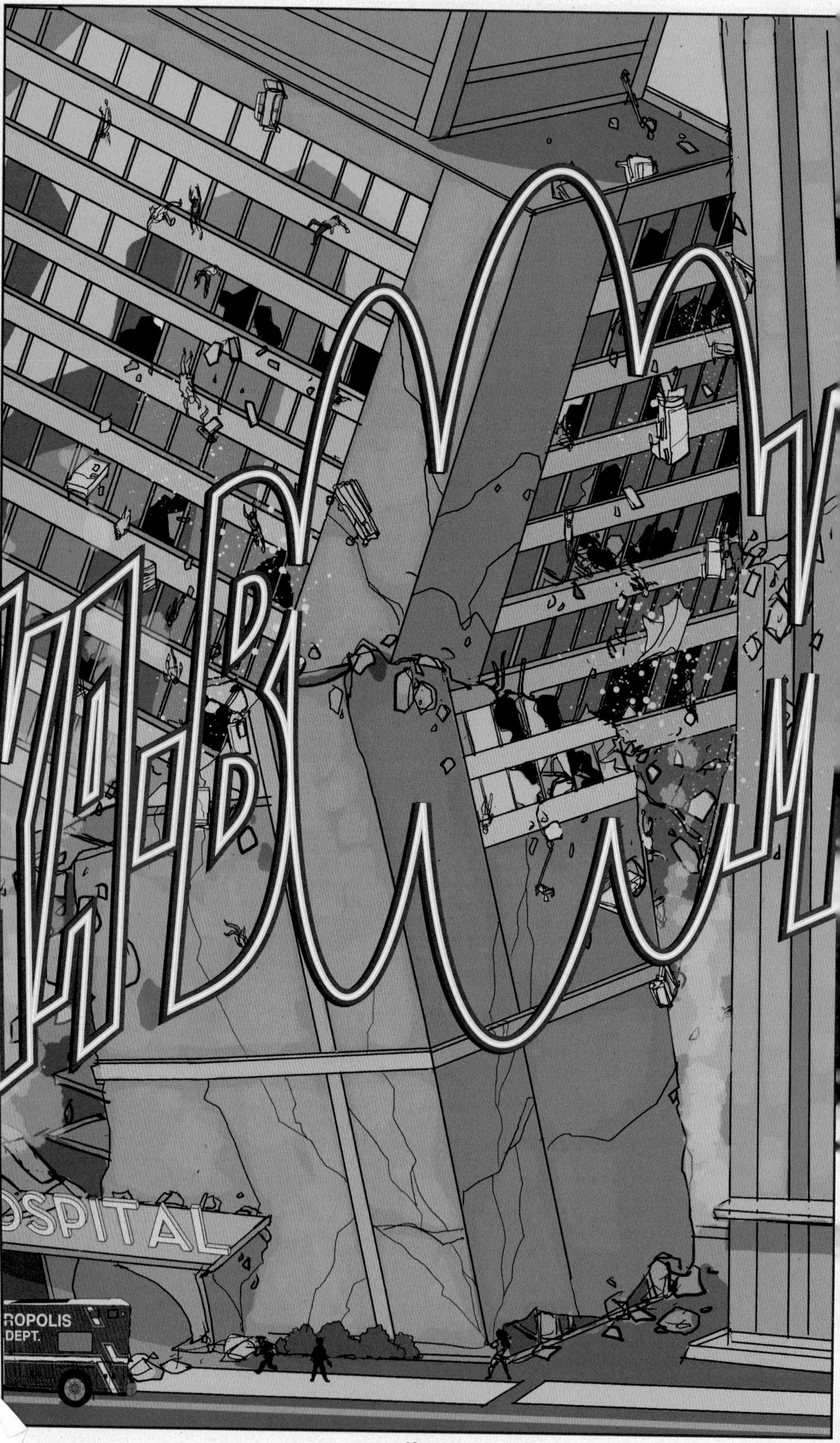
KA-BOOM
OSPITAL
ROPOLIS
DEPT.

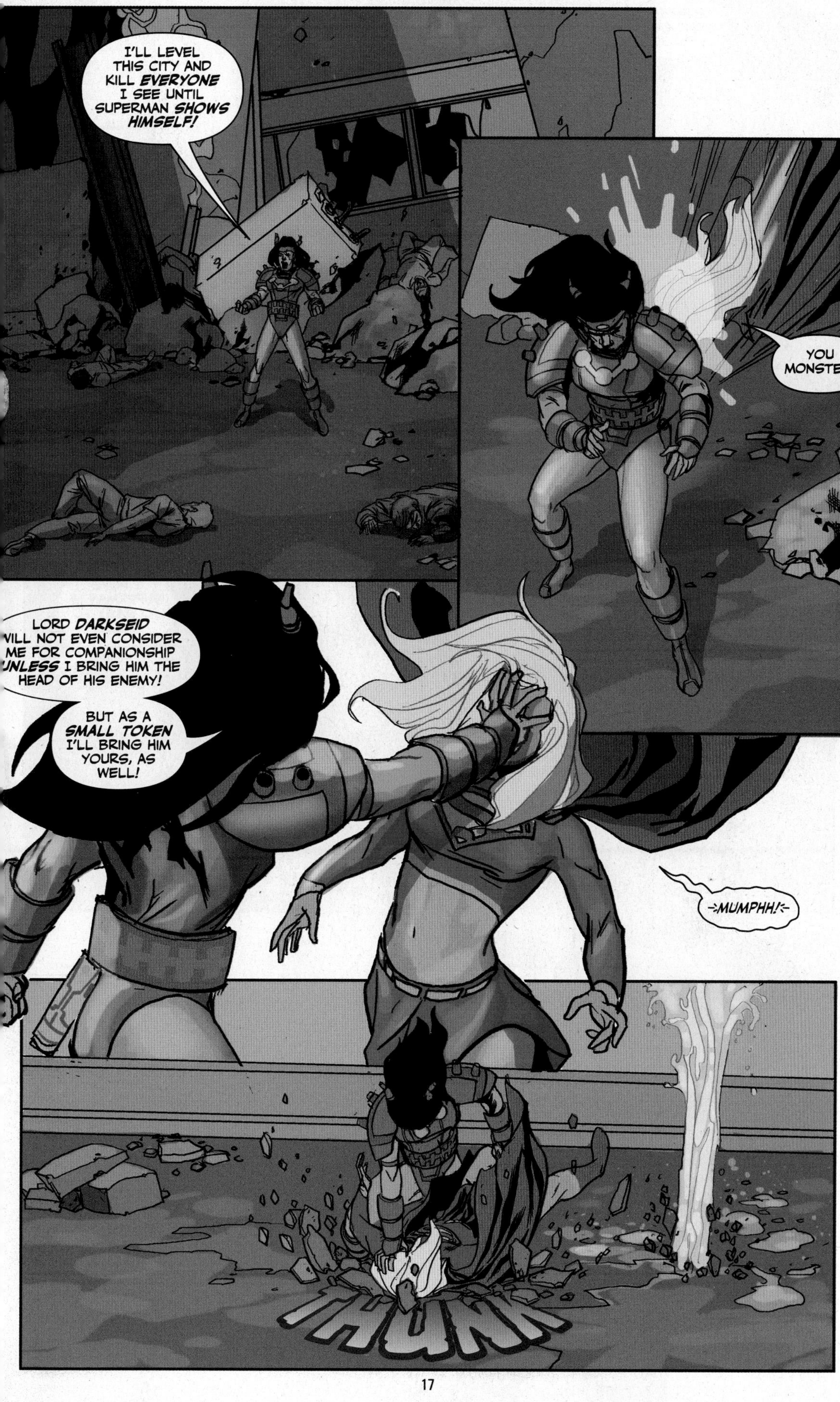
I'LL LEVEL THIS CITY AND KILL EVERYONE I SEE UNTIL SUPERMAN SHOWS HIMSELF!
YOU MONSTER!
LORD DARKSEID WILL NOT EVEN CONSIDER ME FOR COMPANIONSHIP UNLESS I BRING HIM THE HEAD OF HIS ENEMY!
BUT AS A SMALL TOKEN I'LL BRING HIM YOURS, AS WELL!
-MUMPHH!-
THUNK

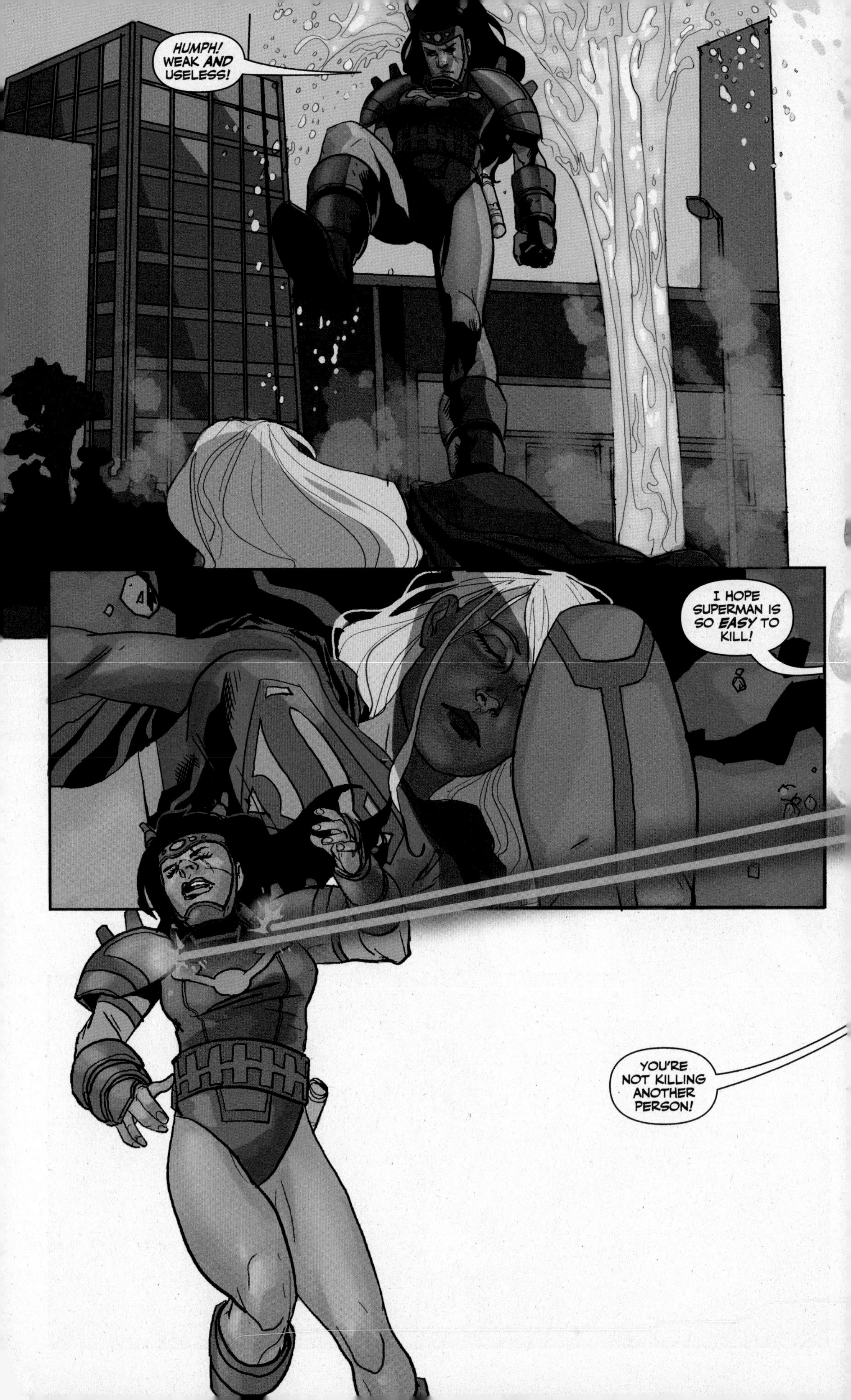
HUMPH! WEAK AND USELESS!
I HOPE SUPERMAN IS SO EASY TO KILL!
YOU'RE NOT KILLING ANOTHER PERSON!

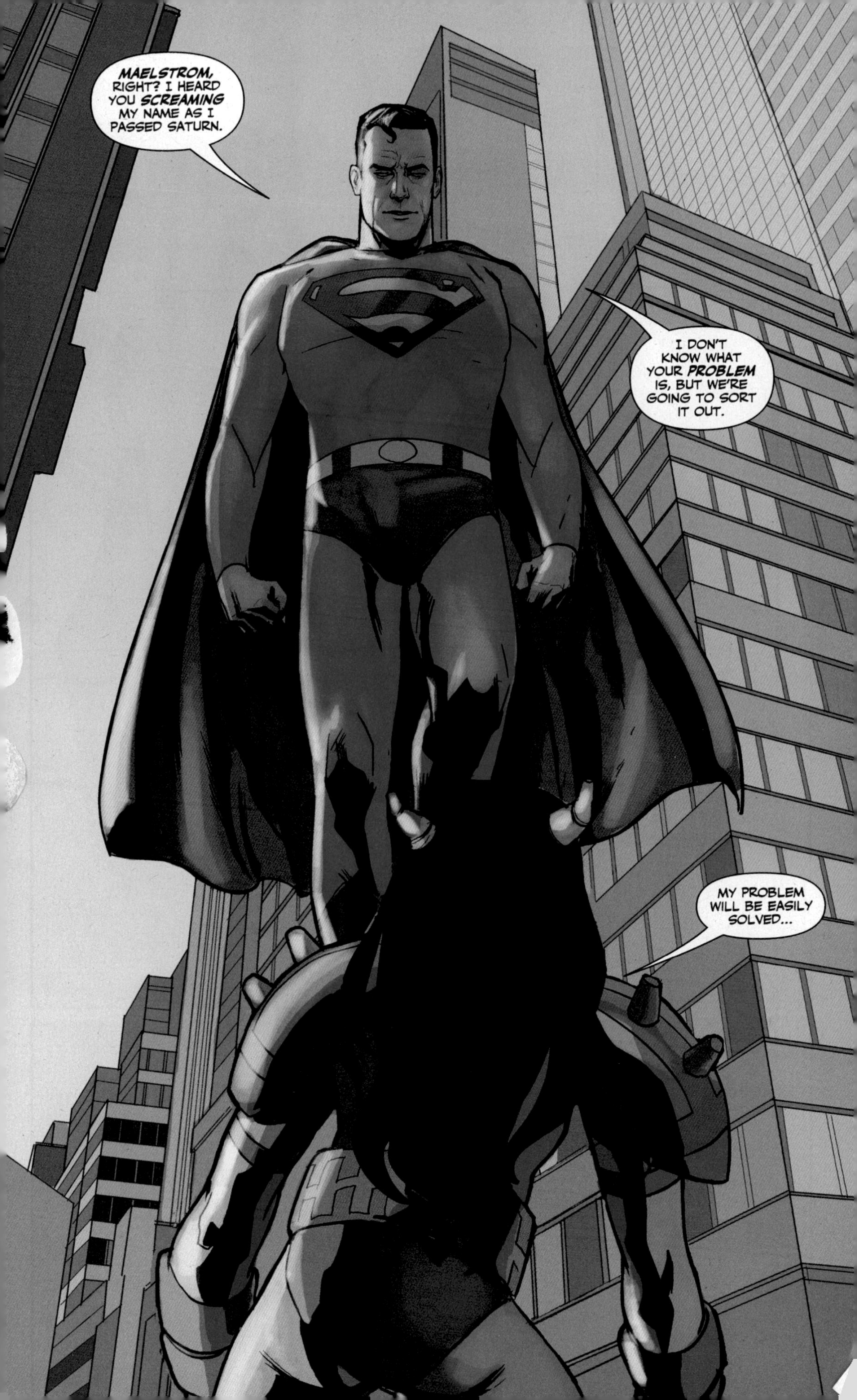
MAELSTROM, RIGHT? I HEARD YOU SCREAMING MY NAME AS I PASSED SATURN.
I DON'T KNOW WHAT YOUR PROBLEM IS, BUT WE'RE GOING TO SORT IT OUT.
MY PROBLEM WILL BE EASILY SOLVED...

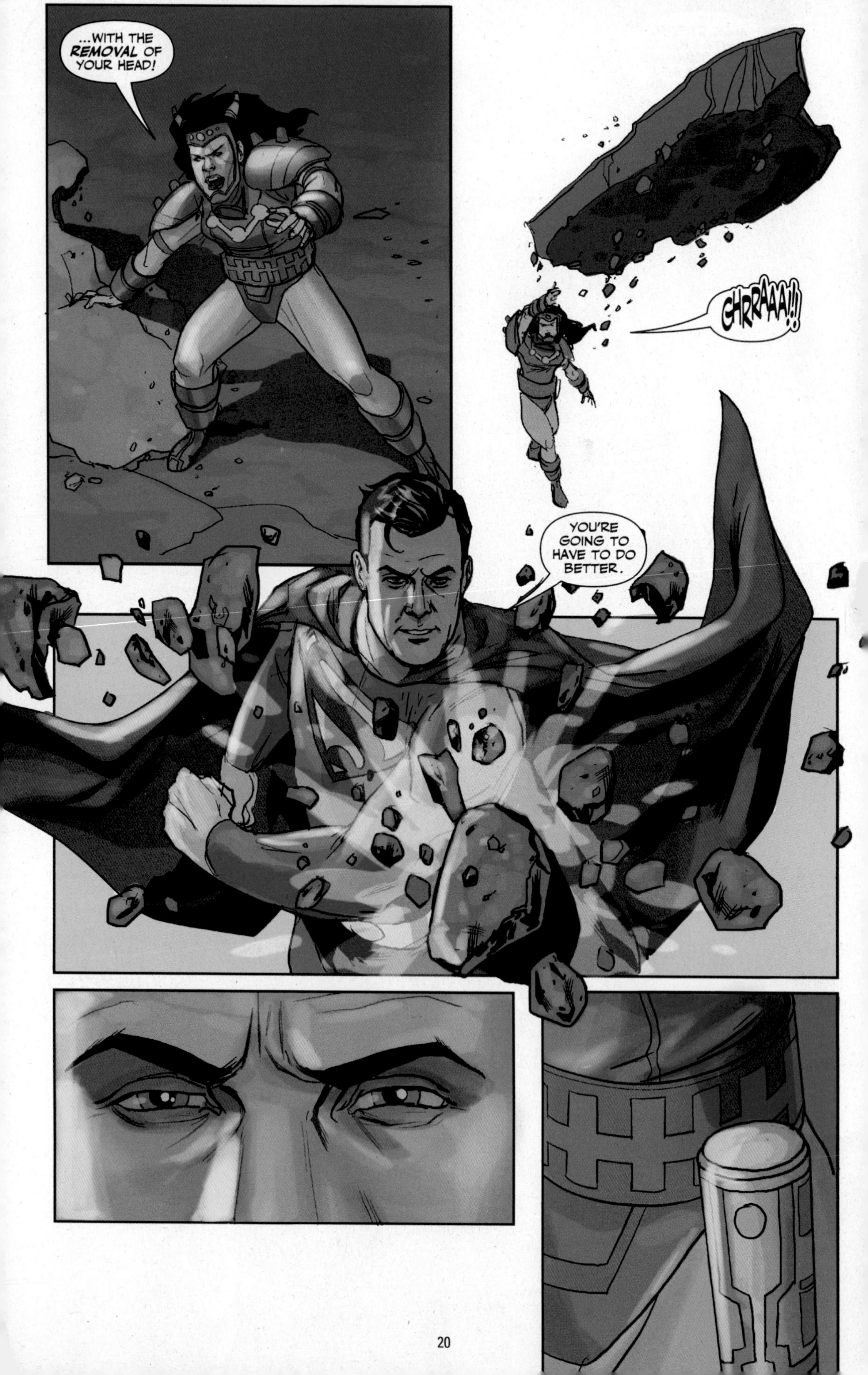
...WITH THE REMOVAL OF YOUR HEAD!
GHRRAAA!!!
YOU'RE GOING TO HAVE TO DO BETTER.

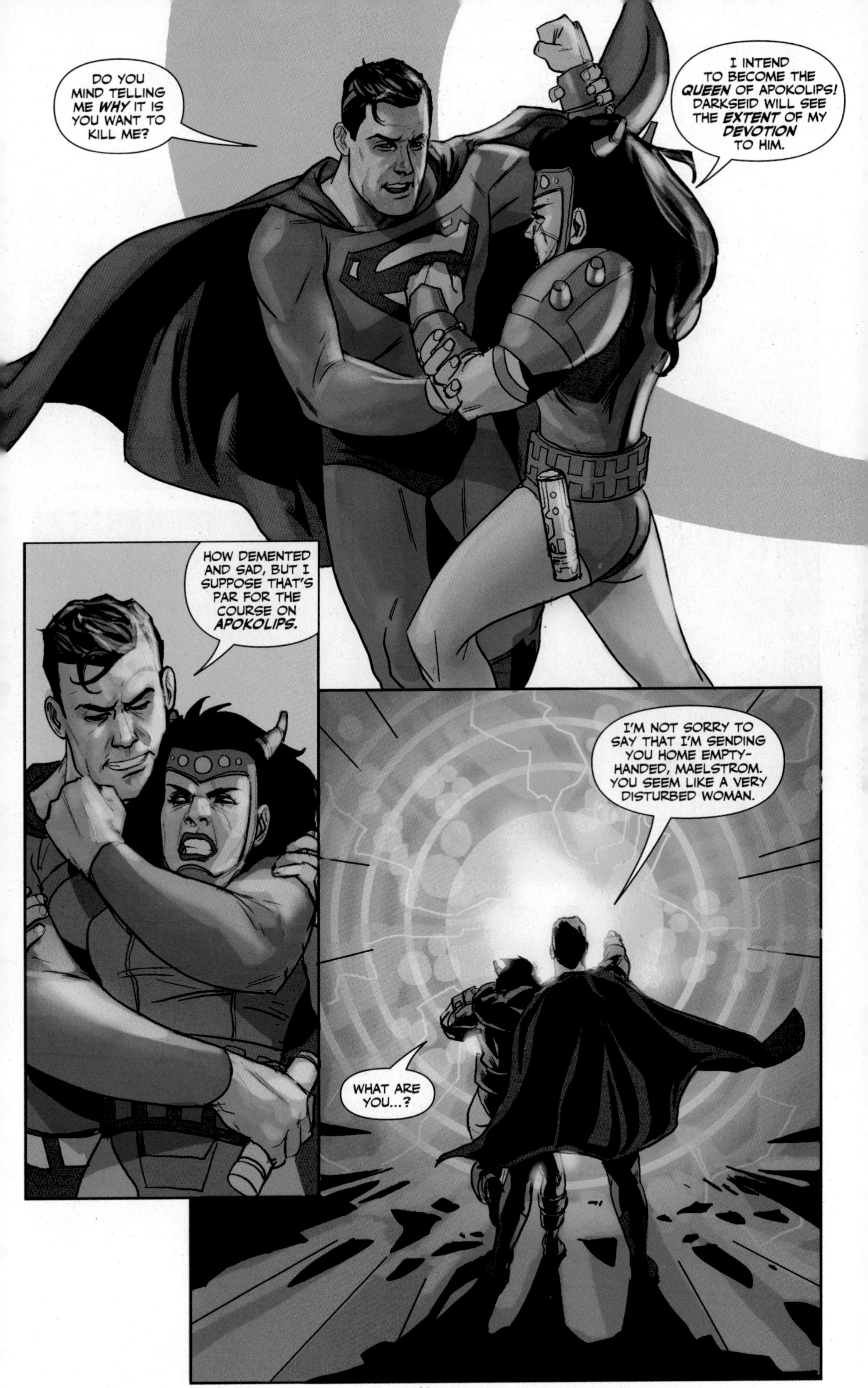
DO YOU MIND TELLING ME WHY IT IS YOU WANT TO KILL ME?
I INTEND TO BECOME THE QUEEN OF APOKOLIPS! DARKSEID WILL SEE THE EXTENT OF MY DEVOTION TO HIM.
HOW DEMENTED AND SAD, BUT I SUPPOSE THAT'S PAR FOR THE COURSE ON APOKOLIPS.
I'M NOT SORRY TO SAY THAT I'M SENDING YOU HOME EMPTY-HANDED, MAELSTROM. YOU SEEM LIKE A VERY DISTURBED WOMAN.
WHAT ARE YOU...?

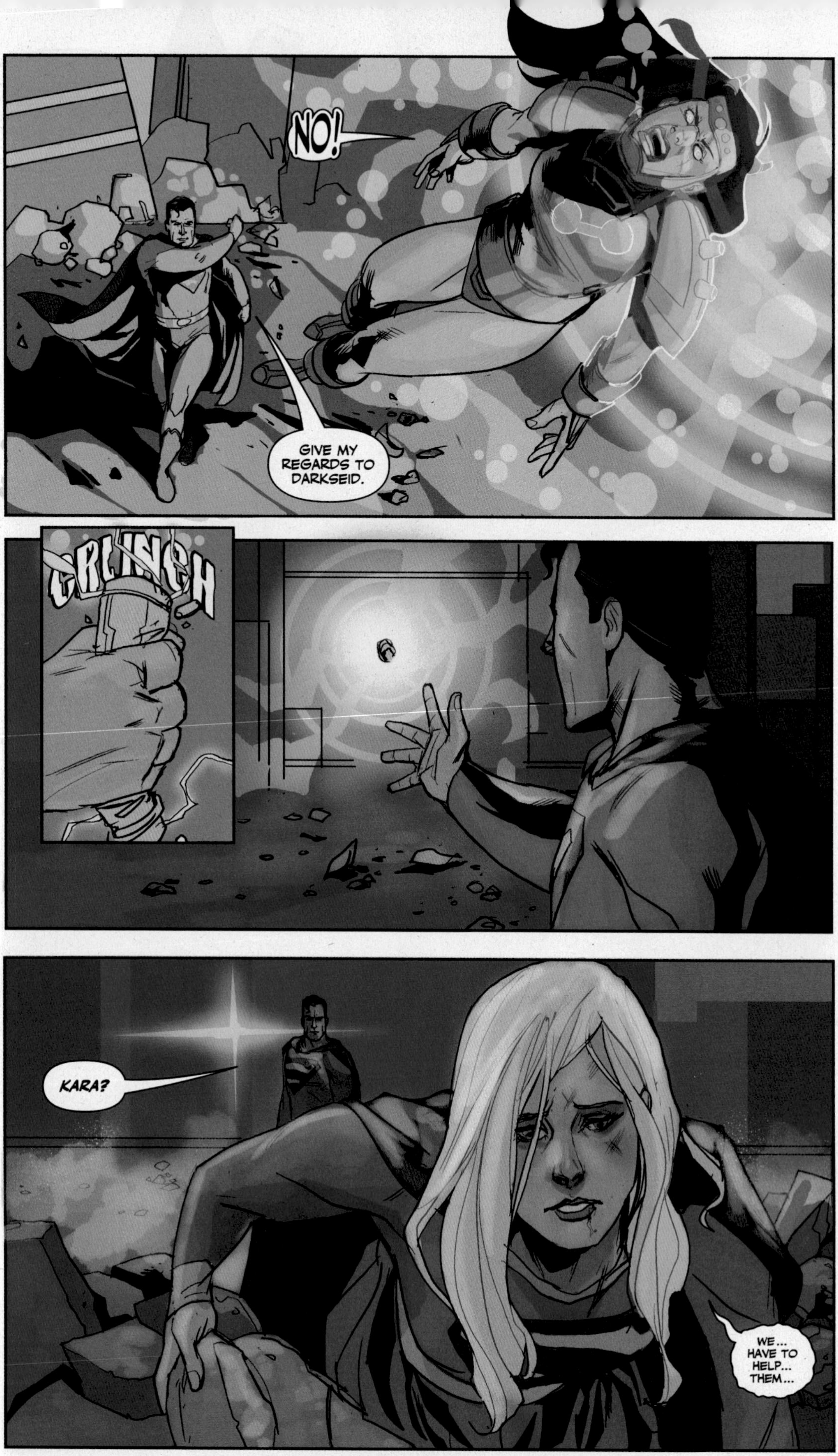
NO!
GIVE MY REGARDS TO DARKSEID.
CRUNCH
KARA?
WE... HAVE TO HELP... THEM...

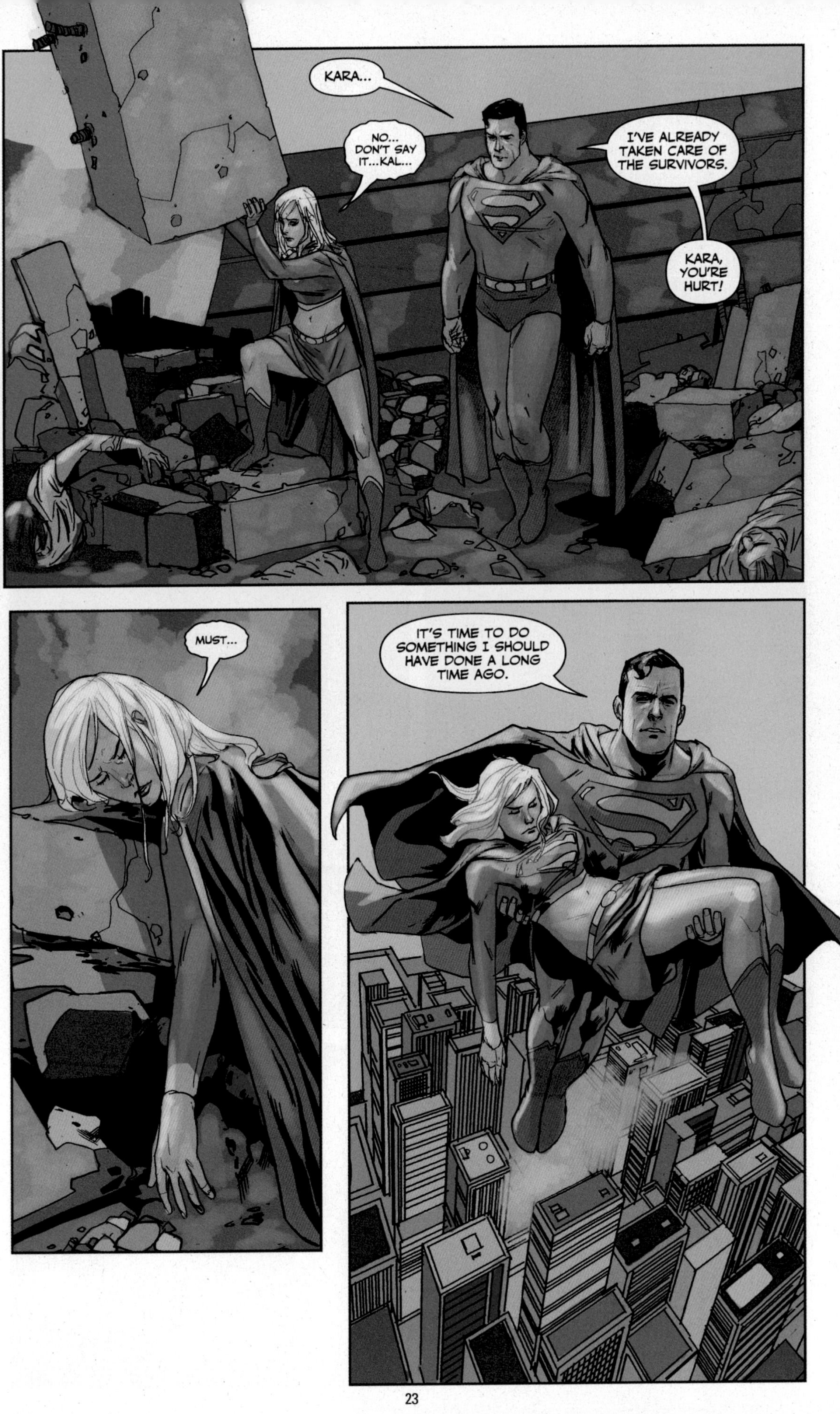
KARA...
NO... DON'T SAY IT...KAL...
I'VE ALREADY TAKEN CARE OF THE SURVIVORS.
KARA, YOU'RE HURT!
MUST...
IT'S TIME TO DO SOMETHING I SHOULD HAVE DONE A LONG TIME AGO.

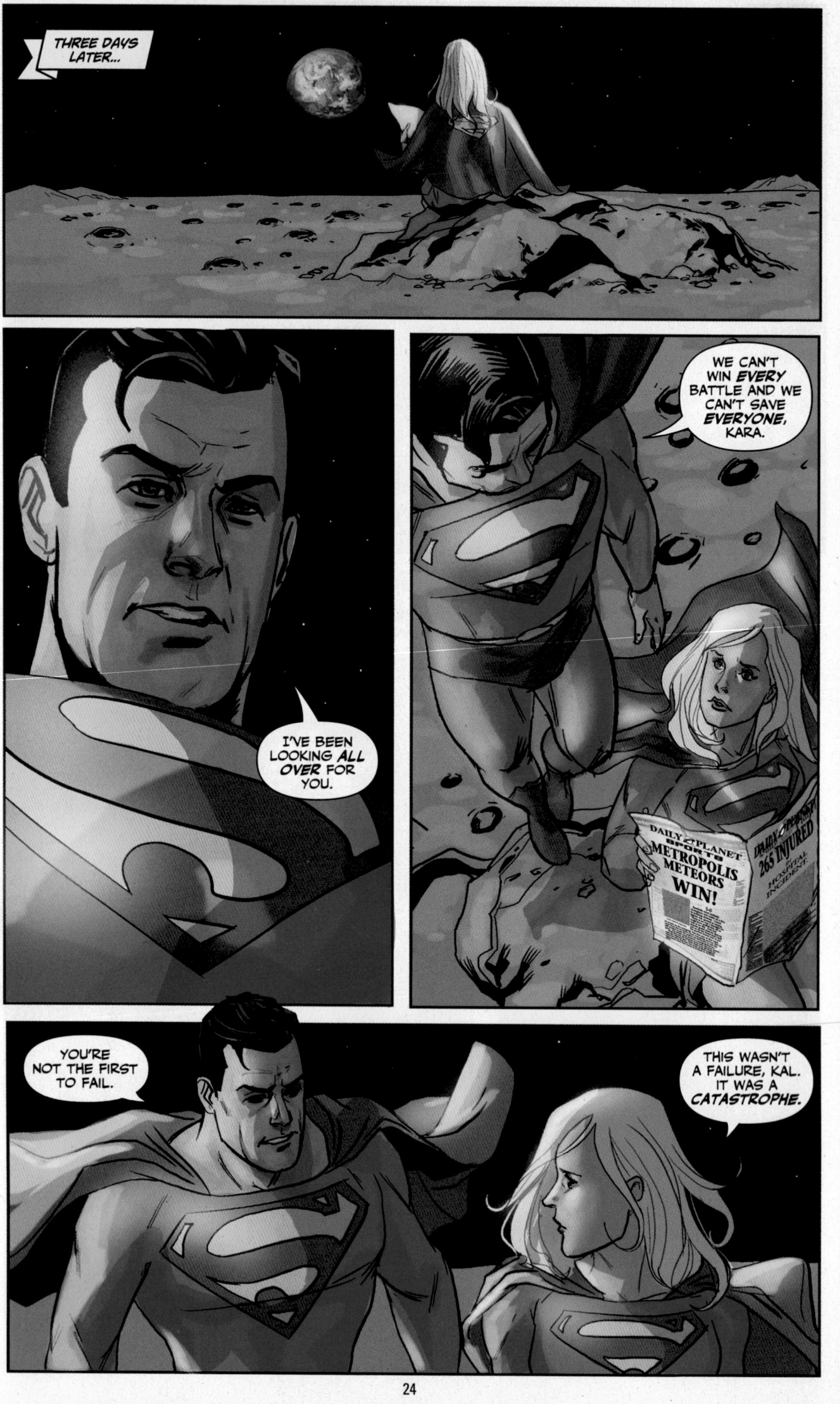

THREE DAYS LATER...
I'VE BEEN LOOKING ALL OVER FOR YOU.
WE CAN'T WIN EVERY BATTLE AND WE CAN'T SAVE EVERYONE, KARA.
DAILY PLANET
SPORTS
METROPOLIS METEORS WIN!
265 INJURED
HOSPITAL INCIDENT
YOU'RE NOT THE FIRST TO FAIL.
THIS WASN'T A FAILURE, KAL. IT WAS A CATASTROPHE.

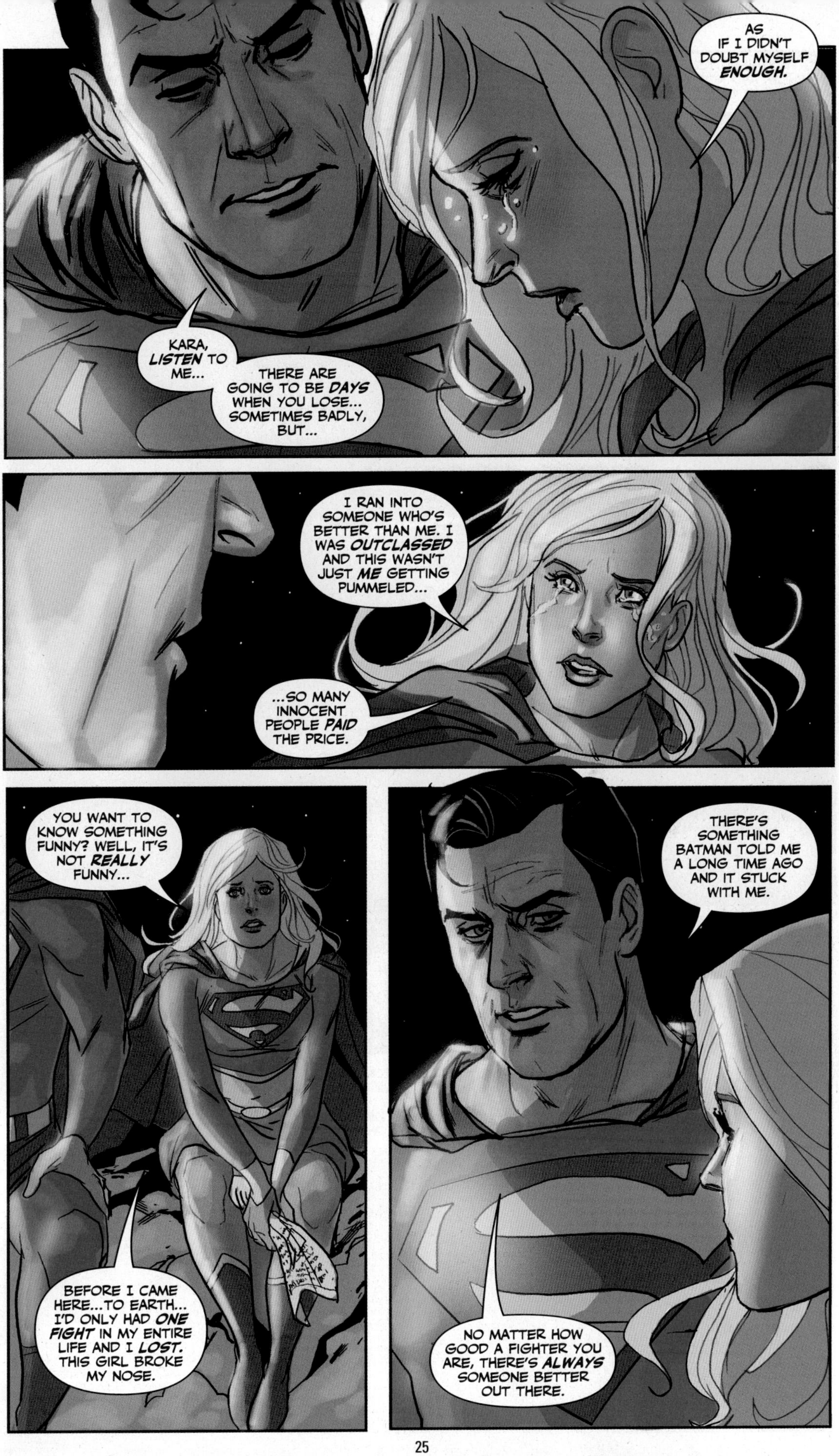
AS IF I DIDN'T DOUBT MYSELF ENOUGH.
KARA, LISTEN TO ME...
THERE ARE GOING TO BE DAYS WHEN YOU LOSE... SOMETIMES BADLY, BUT...
I RAN INTO SOMEONE WHO'S BETTER THAN ME. I WAS OUTCLASSED AND THIS WASN'T JUST ME GETTING PUMMELED...
...SO MANY INNOCENT PEOPLE PAID THE PRICE.
YOU WANT TO KNOW SOMETHING FUNNY? WELL, IT'S NOT REALLY FUNNY...
BEFORE I CAME HERE...TO EARTH... I'D ONLY HAD ONE FIGHT IN MY ENTIRE LIFE AND I LOST. THIS GIRL BROKE MY NOSE.
THERE'S SOMETHING BATMAN TOLD ME A LONG TIME AGO AND IT STUCK WITH ME.
NO MATTER HOW GOOD A FIGHTER YOU ARE, THERE'S ALWAYS SOMEONE BETTER OUT THERE.

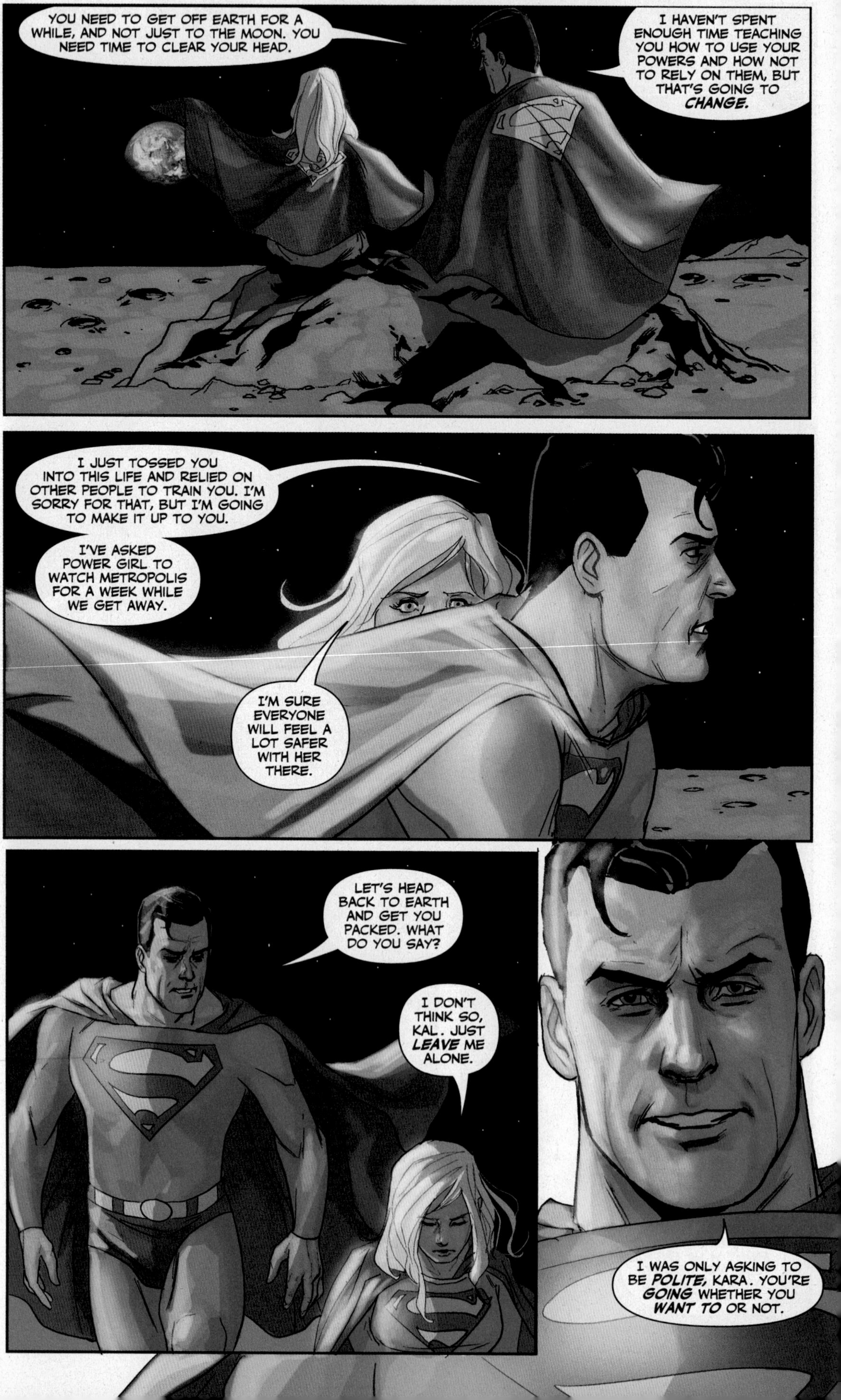
YOU NEED TO GET OFF EARTH FOR A WHILE, AND NOT JUST TO THE MOON. YOU NEED TIME TO CLEAR YOUR HEAD.
I HAVEN'T SPENT ENOUGH TIME TEACHING YOU HOW TO USE YOUR POWERS AND HOW NOT TO RELY ON THEM, BUT THAT'S GOING TO ***CHANGE.***
I JUST TOSSED YOU INTO THIS LIFE AND RELIED ON OTHER PEOPLE TO TRAIN YOU. I'M SORRY FOR THAT, BUT I'M GOING TO MAKE IT UP TO YOU.
I'VE ASKED POWER GIRL TO WATCH METROPOLIS FOR A WEEK WHILE WE GET AWAY.
I'M SURE EVERYONE WILL FEEL A LOT SAFER WITH HER THERE.
LET'S HEAD BACK TO EARTH AND GET YOU PACKED. WHAT DO YOU SAY?
I DON'T THINK SO, KAL. JUST ***LEAVE*** ME ALONE.
I WAS ONLY ASKING TO BE ***POLITE,*** KARA. YOU'RE ***GOING*** WHETHER YOU ***WANT TO*** OR NOT.

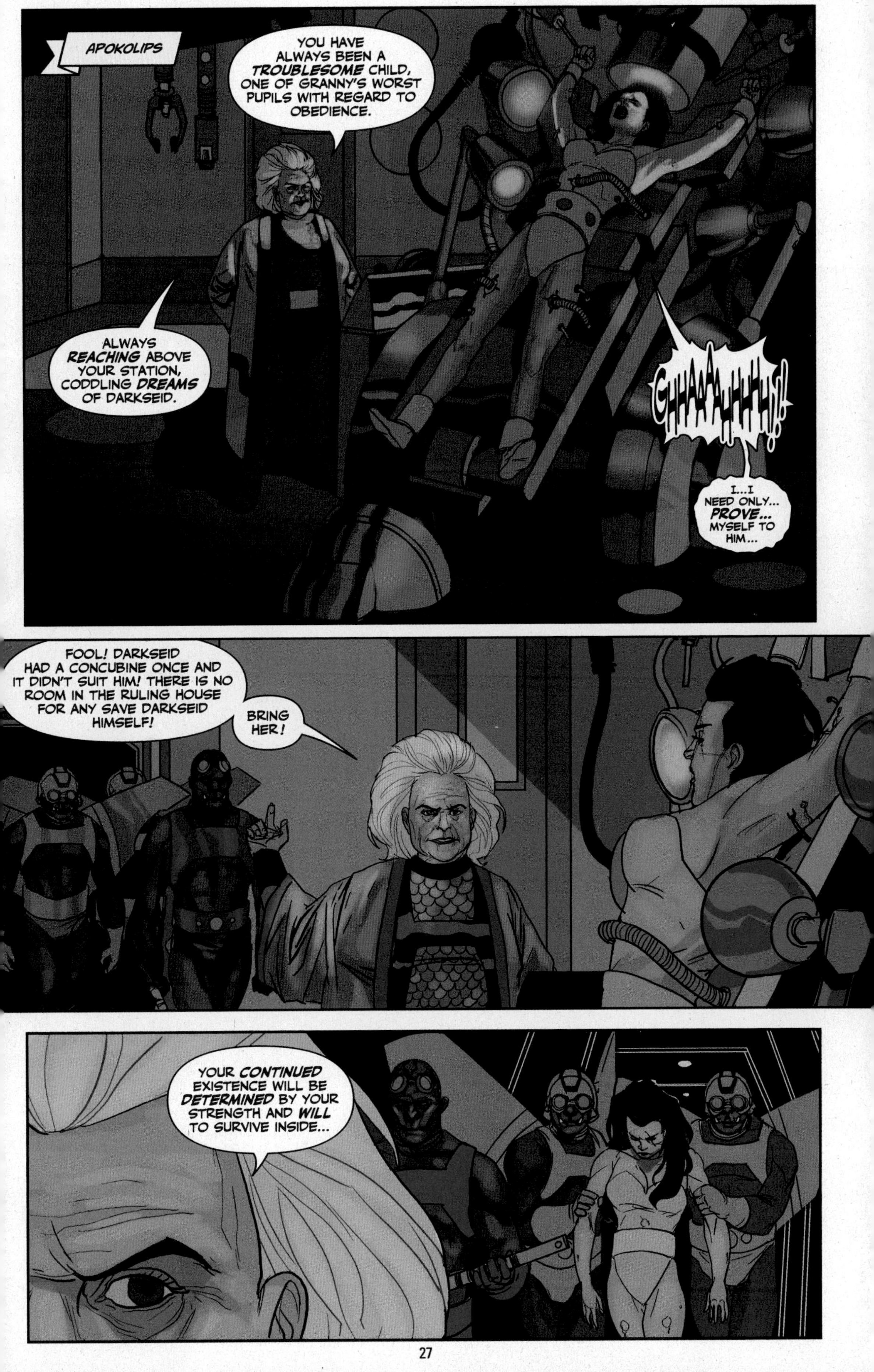
APOKOLIPS
YOU HAVE ALWAYS BEEN A *TROUBLESOME* CHILD, ONE OF GRANNY'S WORST PUPILS WITH REGARD TO OBEDIENCE.
ALWAYS *REACHING* ABOVE YOUR STATION, CODDLING *DREAMS* OF DARKSEID.
GHHAAAAHHHHH!!
I...I NEED ONLY... *PROVE...* MYSELF TO HIM...
FOOL! DARKSEID HAD A CONCUBINE ONCE AND IT DIDN'T SUIT HIM! THERE IS NO ROOM IN THE RULING HOUSE FOR ANY SAVE DARKSEID HIMSELF!
BRING HER!
YOUR *CONTINUED* EXISTENCE WILL BE *DETERMINED* BY YOUR STRENGTH AND *WILL* TO SURVIVE INSIDE...

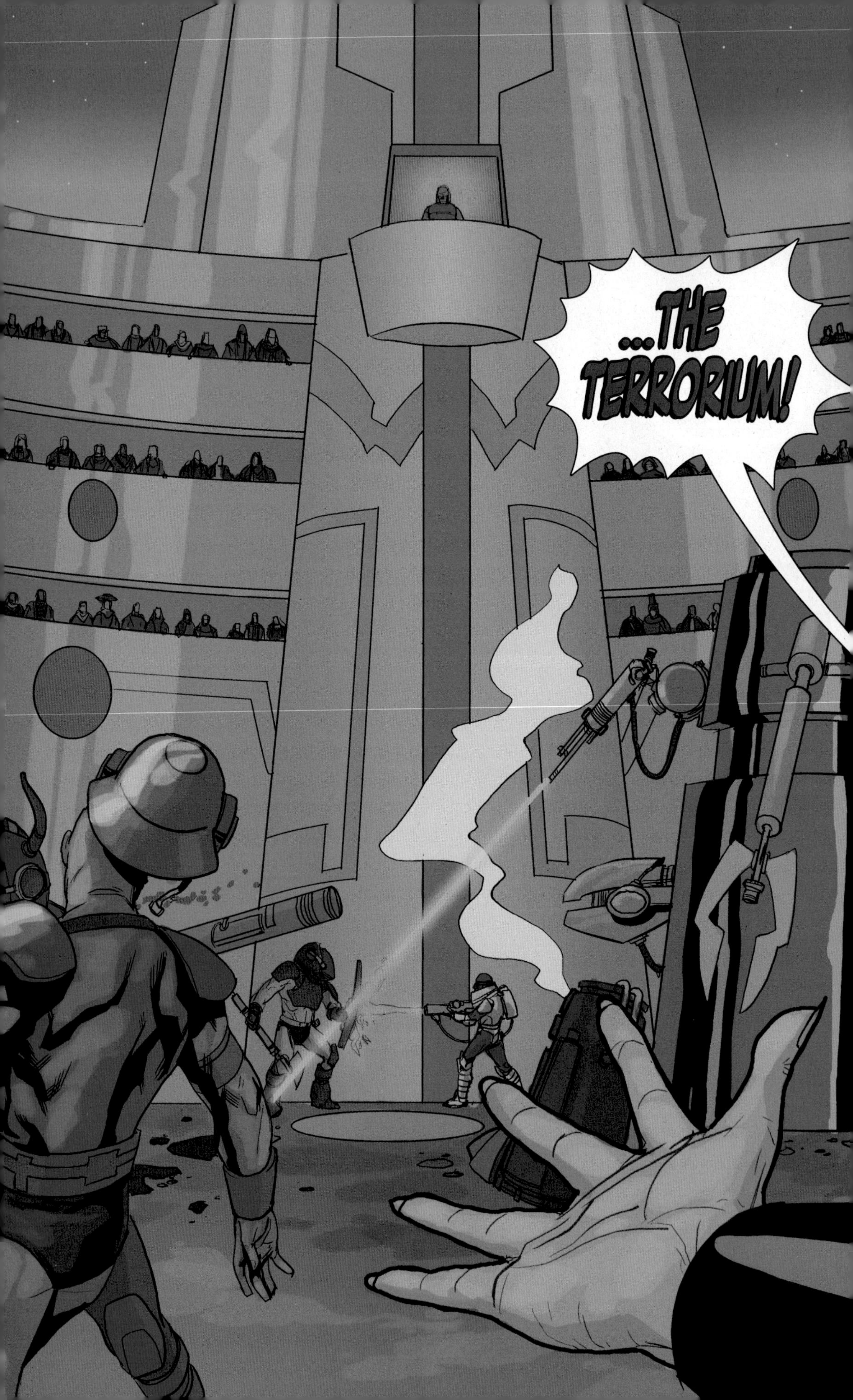
...THE TERRORIUM!

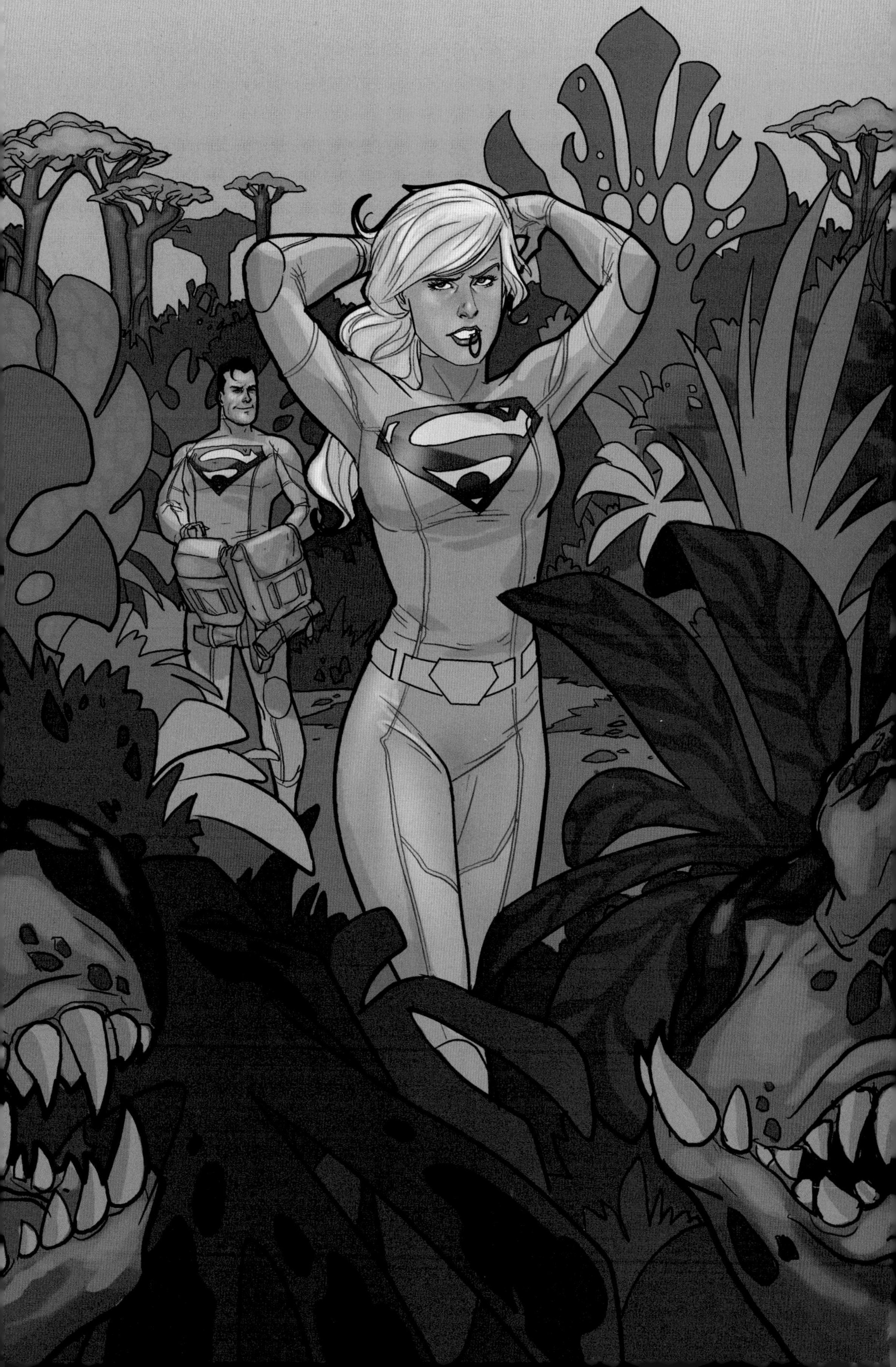

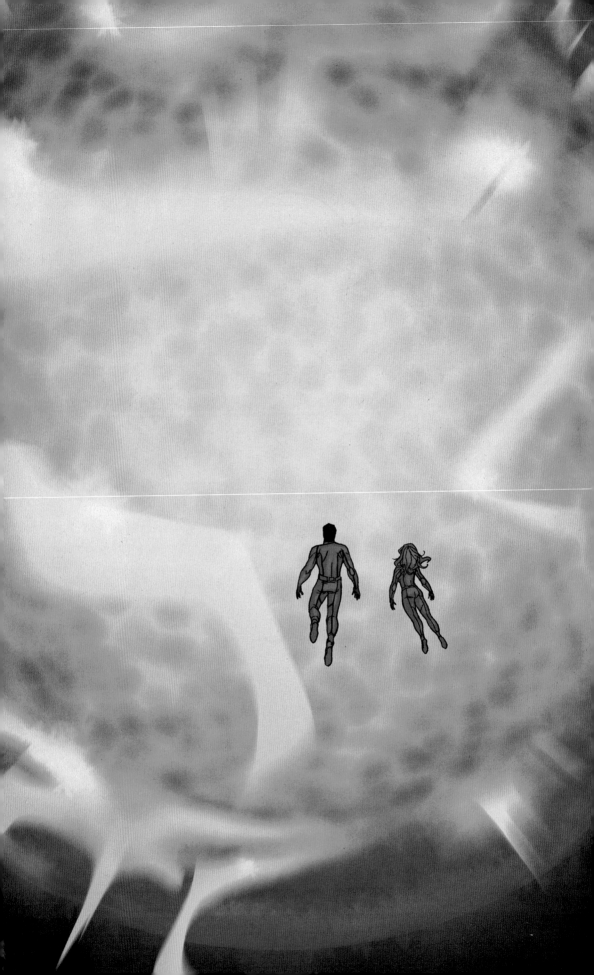

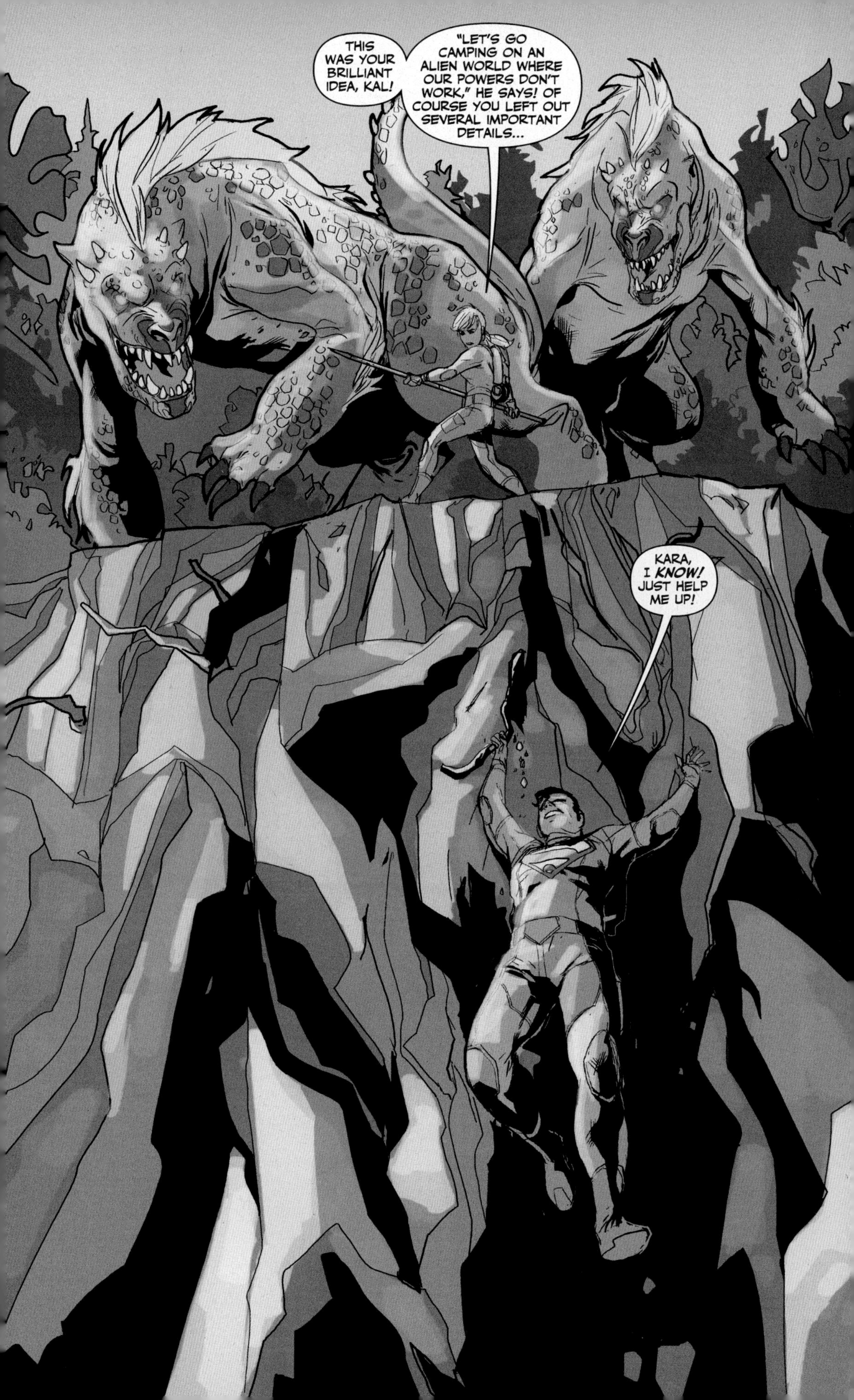
THIS WAS YOUR BRILLIANT IDEA, KAL!
"LET'S GO CAMPING ON AN ALIEN WORLD WHERE OUR POWERS DON'T WORK," HE SAYS! OF COURSE YOU LEFT OUT SEVERAL IMPORTANT DETAILS...
KARA, I *KNOW!* JUST HELP ME UP!

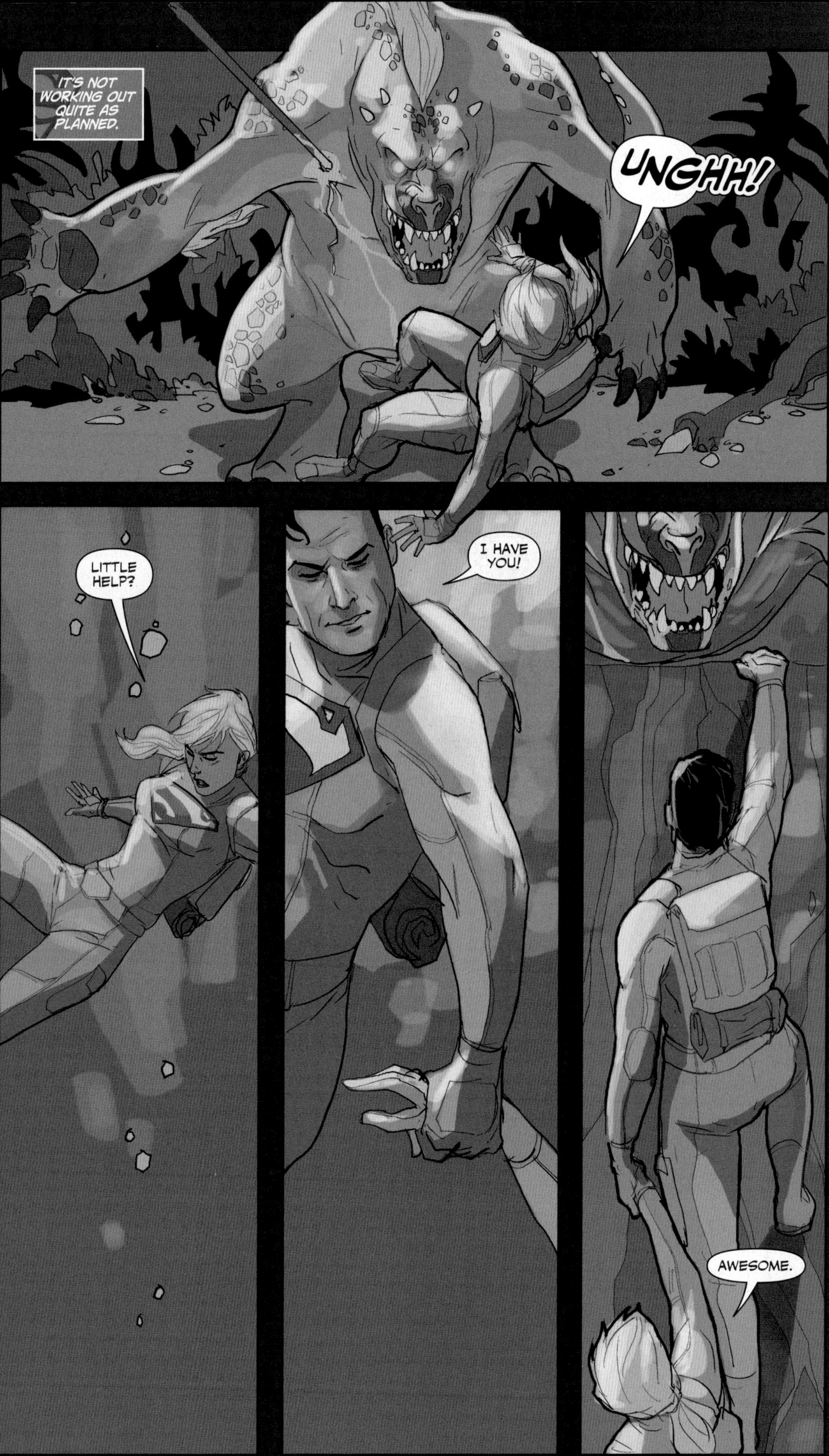
IT'S NOT WORKING OUT QUITE AS PLANNED.
UNGHH!
LITTLE HELP?
I HAVE YOU!
AWESOME.

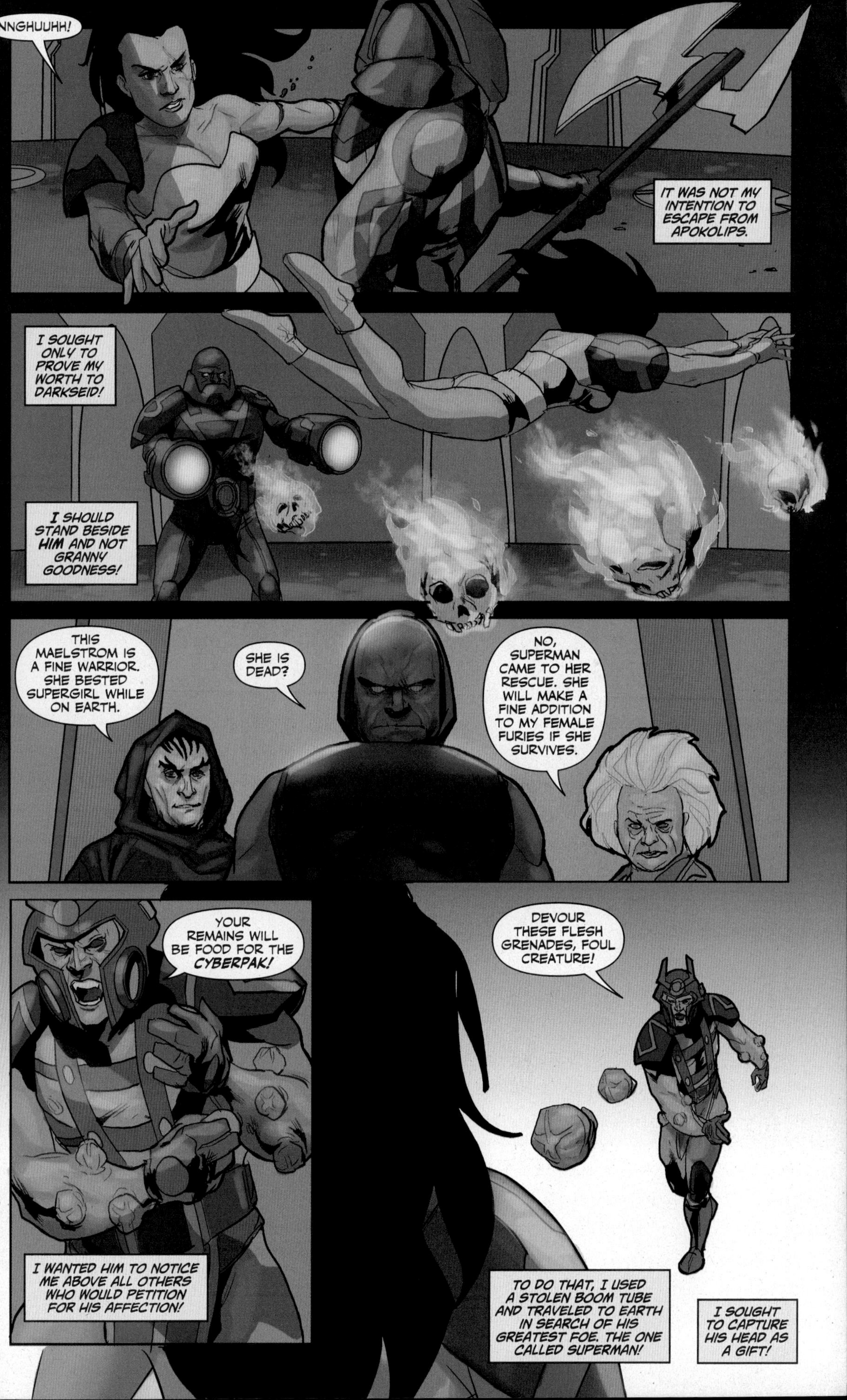
NNGHUUHH!
IT WAS NOT MY INTENTION TO ESCAPE FROM APOKOLIPS.
I SOUGHT ONLY TO PROVE MY WORTH TO DARKSEID!
I SHOULD STAND BESIDE HIM AND NOT GRANNY GOODNESS!
THIS MAELSTROM IS A FINE WARRIOR. SHE BESTED SUPERGIRL WHILE ON EARTH.
SHE IS DEAD?
NO, SUPERMAN CAME TO HER RESCUE. SHE WILL MAKE A FINE ADDITION TO MY FEMALE FURIES IF SHE SURVIVES.
YOUR REMAINS WILL BE FOOD FOR THE CYBERPAK!
DEVOUR THESE FLESH GRENADES, FOUL CREATURE!
I WANTED HIM TO NOTICE ME ABOVE ALL OTHERS WHO WOULD PETITION FOR HIS AFFECTION!
TO DO THAT, I USED A STOLEN BOOM TUBE AND TRAVELED TO EARTH IN SEARCH OF HIS GREATEST FOE. THE ONE CALLED SUPERMAN!
I SOUGHT TO CAPTURE HIS HEAD AS A GIFT!

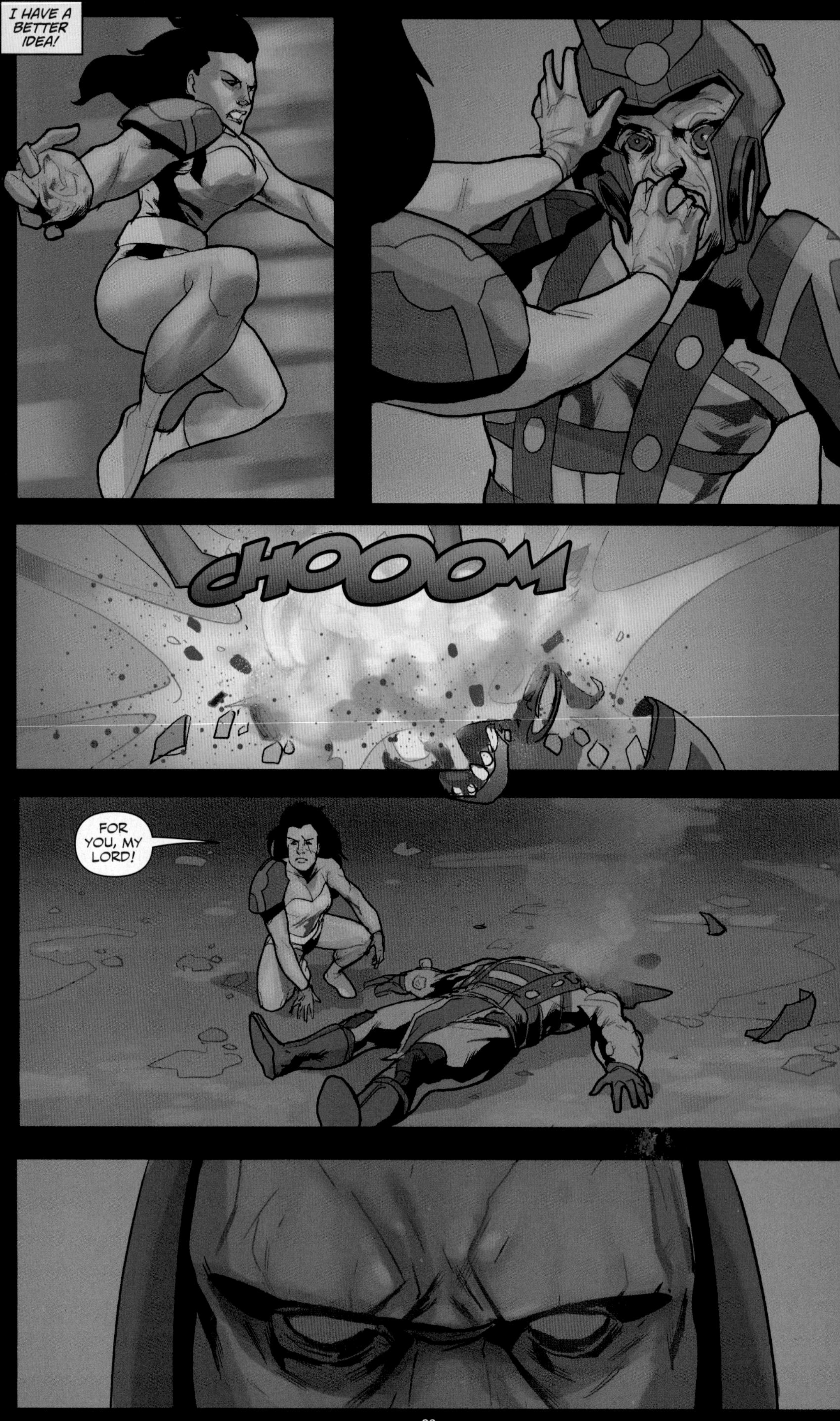
I HAVE A BETTER IDEA!
CHOOOM
FOR YOU, MY LORD!

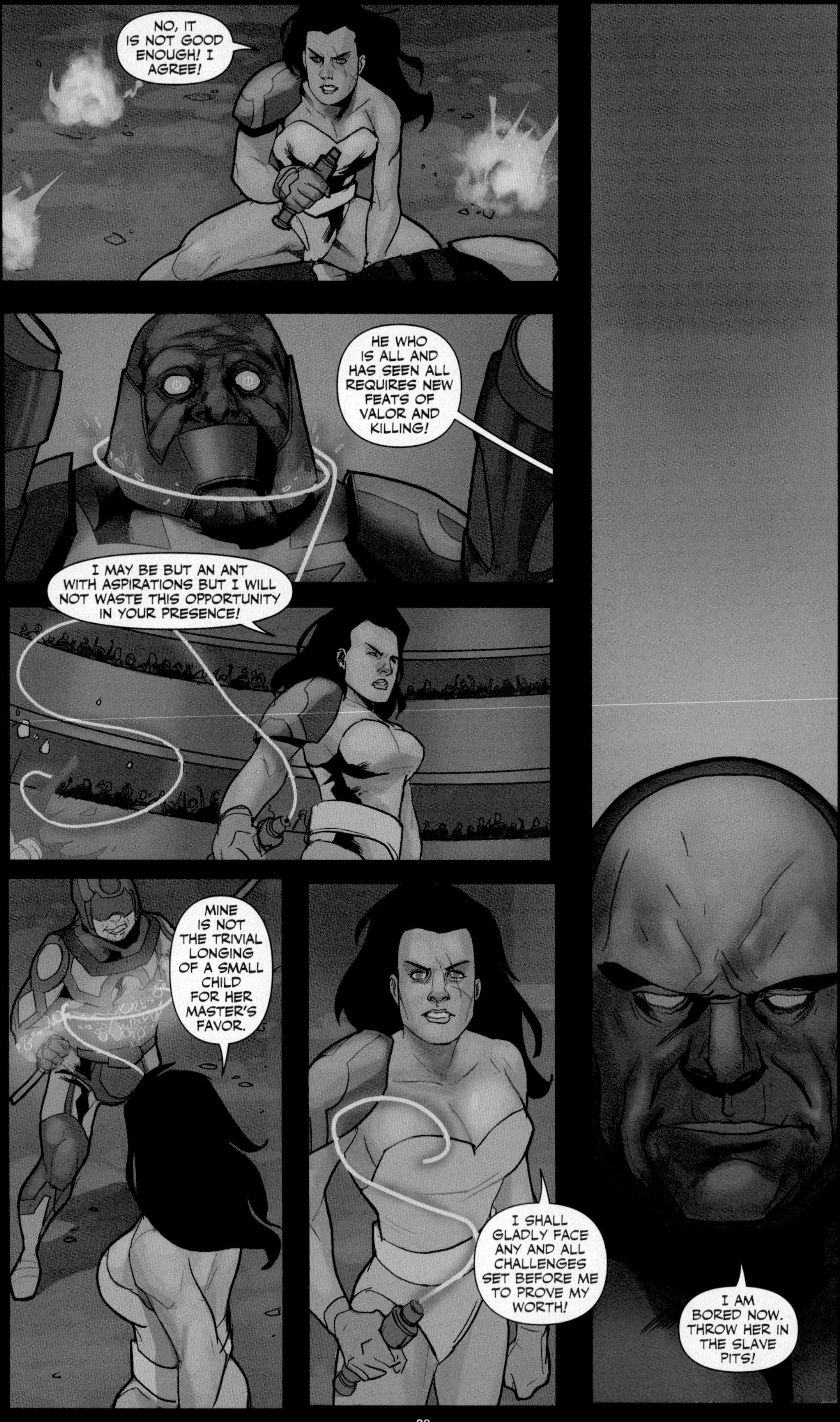
NO, IT IS NOT GOOD ENOUGH! I AGREE!
HE WHO IS ALL AND HAS SEEN ALL REQUIRES NEW FEATS OF VALOR AND KILLING!
I MAY BE BUT AN ANT WITH ASPIRATIONS BUT I WILL NOT WASTE THIS OPPORTUNITY IN YOUR PRESENCE!
MINE IS NOT THE TRIVIAL LONGING OF A SMALL CHILD FOR HER MASTER'S FAVOR.
I SHALL GLADLY FACE ANY AND ALL CHALLENGES SET BEFORE ME TO PROVE MY WORTH!
I AM BORED NOW. THROW HER IN THE SLAVE PITS!

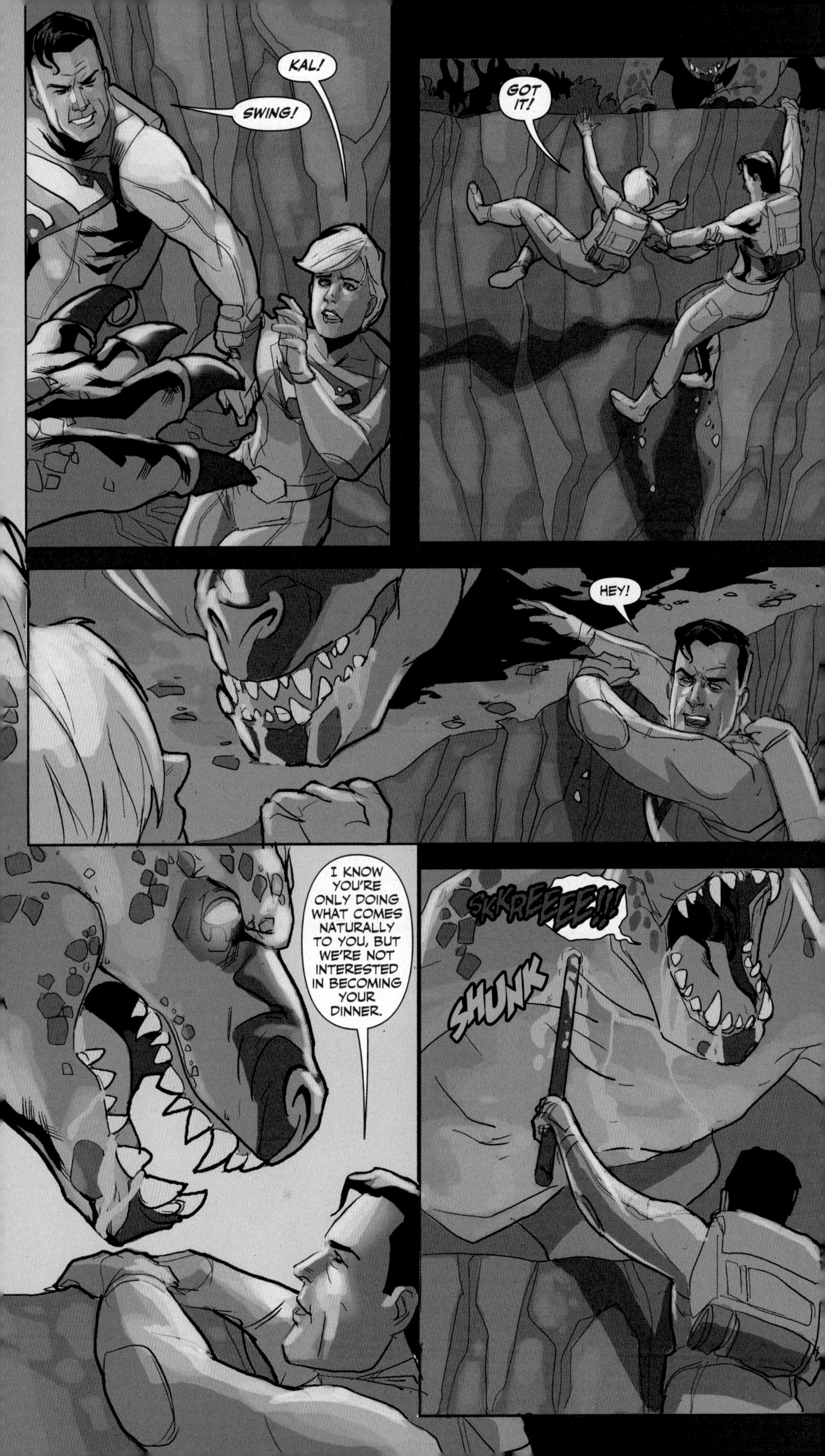

KAL!
SWING!
GOT IT!
HEY!
I KNOW YOU'RE ONLY DOING WHAT COMES NATURALLY TO YOU, BUT WE'RE NOT INTERESTED IN BECOMING YOUR DINNER.
SKKREEEE!!!
SHUNK

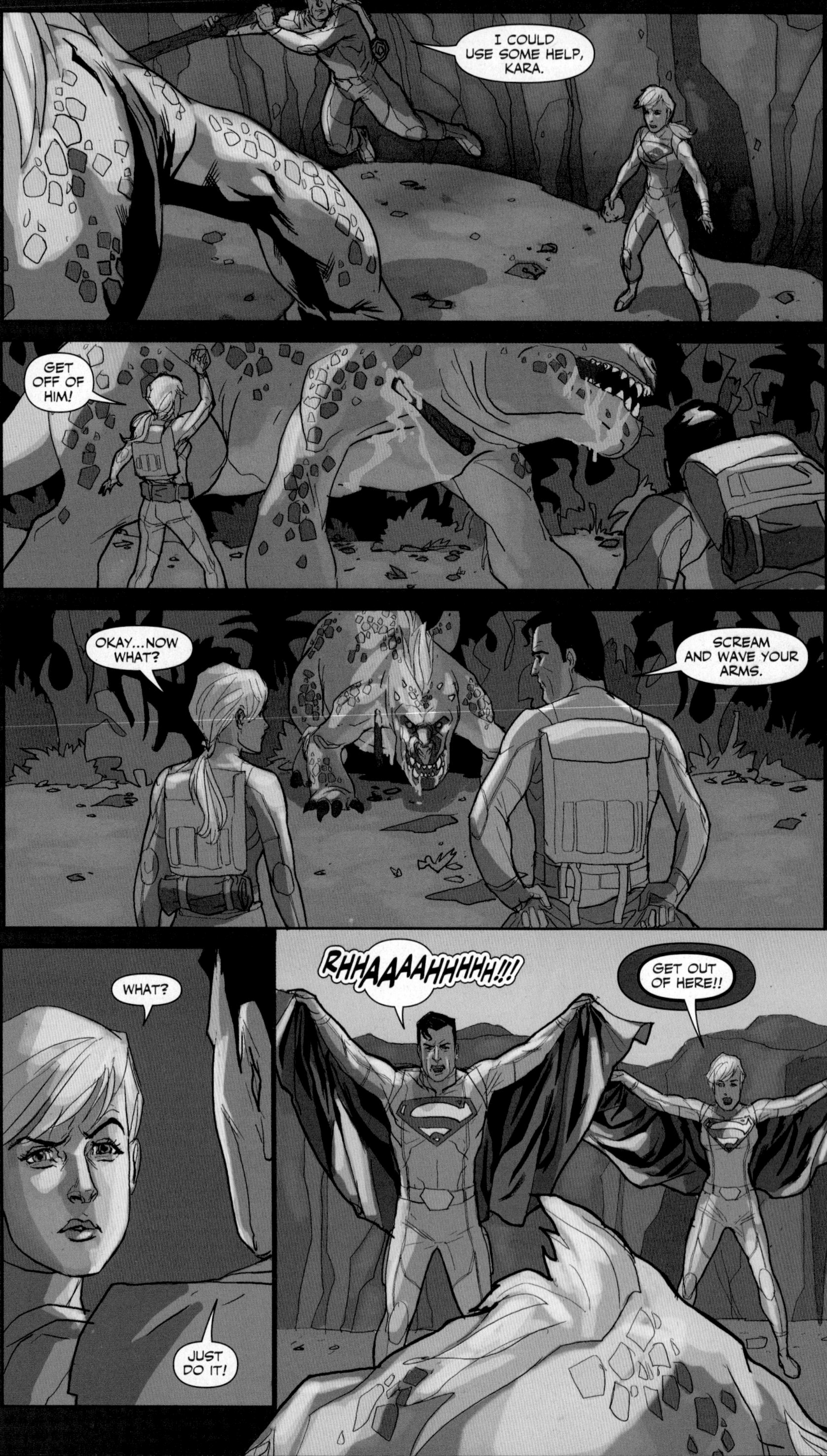
I COULD USE SOME HELP, KARA.
GET OFF OF HIM!
OKAY...NOW WHAT?
SCREAM AND WAVE YOUR ARMS.
WHAT?
JUST DO IT!
RHHAAAAHHHHH!!!
GET OUT OF HERE!!

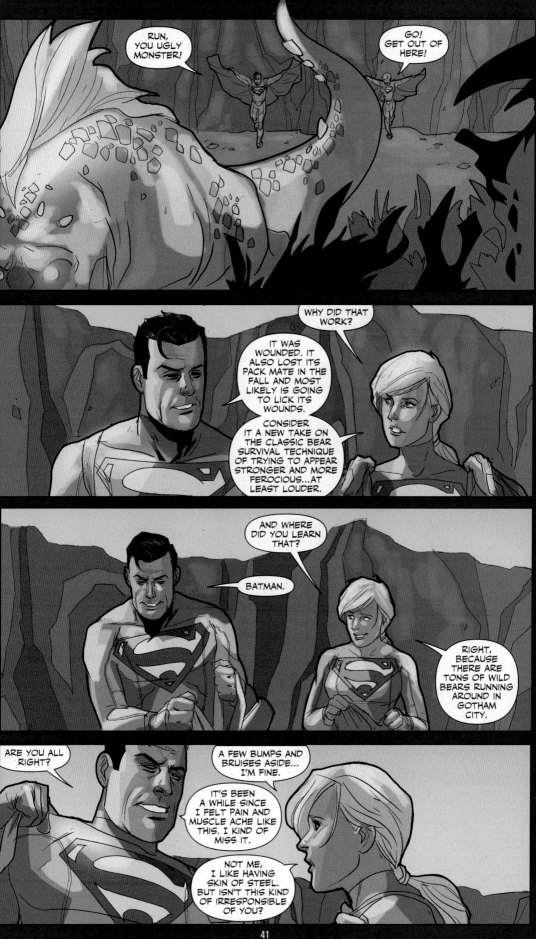

RUN, YOU UGLY MONSTER!

GO! GET OUT OF HERE!

WHY DID THAT WORK?

IT WAS WOUNDED. IT ALSO LOST ITS PACK MATE IN THE FALL AND MOST LIKELY IS GOING TO LICK ITS WOUNDS.

CONSIDER IT A NEW TAKE ON THE CLASSIC BEAR SURVIVAL TECHNIQUE OF TRYING TO APPEAR STRONGER AND MORE FEROCIOUS...AT LEAST LOUDER.

AND WHERE DID YOU LEARN THAT?

BATMAN.

RIGHT, BECAUSE THERE ARE TONS OF WILD BEARS RUNNING AROUND IN GOTHAM CITY.

ARE YOU ALL RIGHT?

A FEW BUMPS AND BRUISES ASIDE... I'M FINE.

IT'S BEEN A WHILE SINCE I FELT PAIN AND MUSCLE ACHE LIKE THIS. I KIND OF MISS IT.

NOT ME, I LIKE HAVING SKIN OF STEEL. BUT ISN'T THIS KIND OF IRRESPONSIBLE OF YOU?

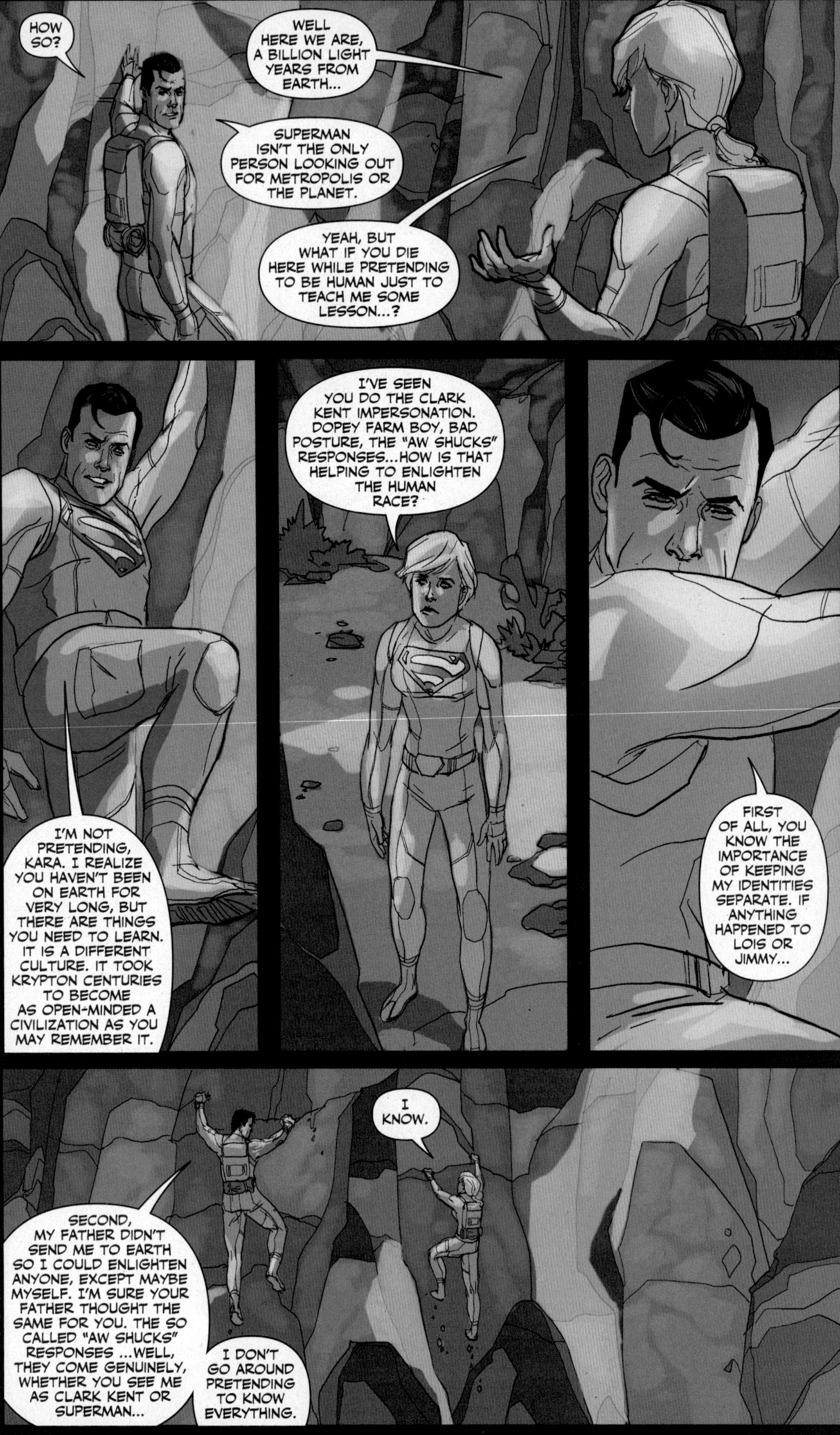
HOW SO?
WELL HERE WE ARE, A BILLION LIGHT YEARS FROM EARTH...
SUPERMAN ISN'T THE ONLY PERSON LOOKING OUT FOR METROPOLIS OR THE PLANET.
YEAH, BUT WHAT IF YOU DIE HERE WHILE PRETENDING TO BE HUMAN JUST TO TEACH ME SOME LESSON...?
I'VE SEEN YOU DO THE CLARK KENT IMPERSONATION. DOPEY FARM BOY, BAD POSTURE, THE "AW SHUCKS" RESPONSES...HOW IS THAT HELPING TO ENLIGHTEN THE HUMAN RACE?
I'M NOT PRETENDING, KARA. I REALIZE YOU HAVEN'T BEEN ON EARTH FOR VERY LONG, BUT THERE ARE THINGS YOU NEED TO LEARN. IT IS A DIFFERENT CULTURE. IT TOOK KRYPTON CENTURIES TO BECOME AS OPEN-MINDED A CIVILIZATION AS YOU MAY REMEMBER IT.
FIRST OF ALL, YOU KNOW THE IMPORTANCE OF KEEPING MY IDENTITIES SEPARATE. IF ANYTHING HAPPENED TO LOIS OR JIMMY...
I KNOW.
SECOND, MY FATHER DIDN'T SEND ME TO EARTH SO I COULD ENLIGHTEN ANYONE, EXCEPT MAYBE MYSELF. I'M SURE YOUR FATHER THOUGHT THE SAME FOR YOU. THE SO CALLED "AW SHUCKS" RESPONSES ...WELL, THEY COME GENUINELY, WHETHER YOU SEE ME AS CLARK KENT OR SUPERMAN...
I DON'T GO AROUND PRETENDING TO KNOW EVERYTHING.

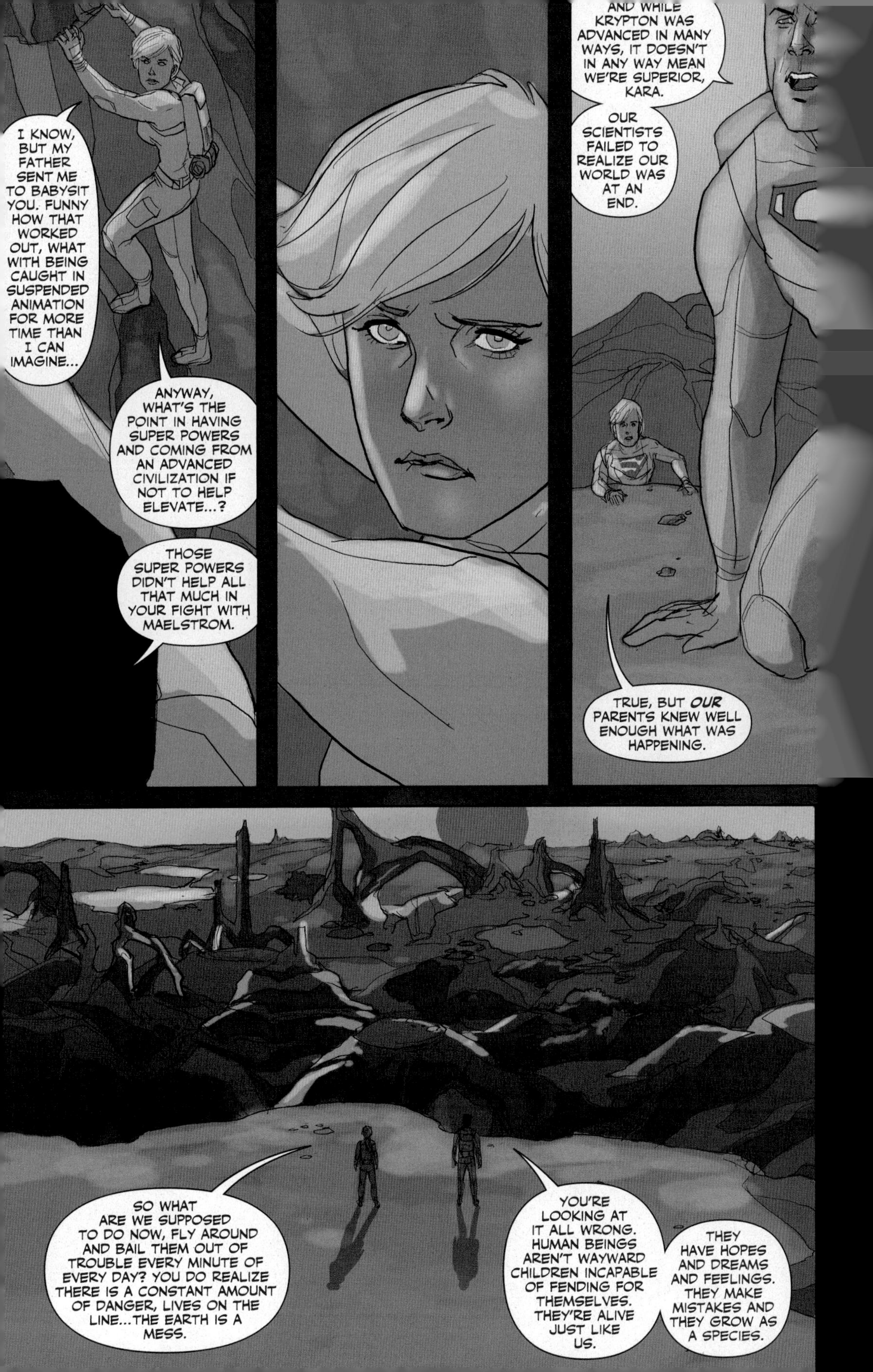
I KNOW, BUT MY FATHER SENT ME TO BABYSIT YOU. FUNNY HOW THAT WORKED OUT, WHAT WITH BEING CAUGHT IN SUSPENDED ANIMATION FOR MORE TIME THAN I CAN IMAGINE...
ANYWAY, WHAT'S THE POINT IN HAVING SUPER POWERS AND COMING FROM AN ADVANCED CIVILIZATION IF NOT TO HELP ELEVATE...?
THOSE SUPER POWERS DIDN'T HELP ALL THAT MUCH IN YOUR FIGHT WITH MAELSTROM.
AND WHILE KRYPTON WAS ADVANCED IN MANY WAYS, IT DOESN'T IN ANY WAY MEAN WE'RE SUPERIOR, KARA.
OUR SCIENTISTS FAILED TO REALIZE OUR WORLD WAS AT AN END.
TRUE, BUT *OUR* PARENTS KNEW WELL ENOUGH WHAT WAS HAPPENING.
SO WHAT ARE WE SUPPOSED TO DO NOW, FLY AROUND AND BAIL THEM OUT OF TROUBLE EVERY MINUTE OF EVERY DAY? YOU DO REALIZE THERE IS A CONSTANT AMOUNT OF DANGER, LIVES ON THE LINE...THE EARTH IS A MESS.
YOU'RE LOOKING AT IT ALL WRONG. HUMAN BEINGS AREN'T WAYWARD CHILDREN INCAPABLE OF FENDING FOR THEMSELVES. THEY'RE ALIVE JUST LIKE US.
THEY HAVE HOPES AND DREAMS AND FEELINGS. THEY MAKE MISTAKES AND THEY GROW AS A SPECIES.

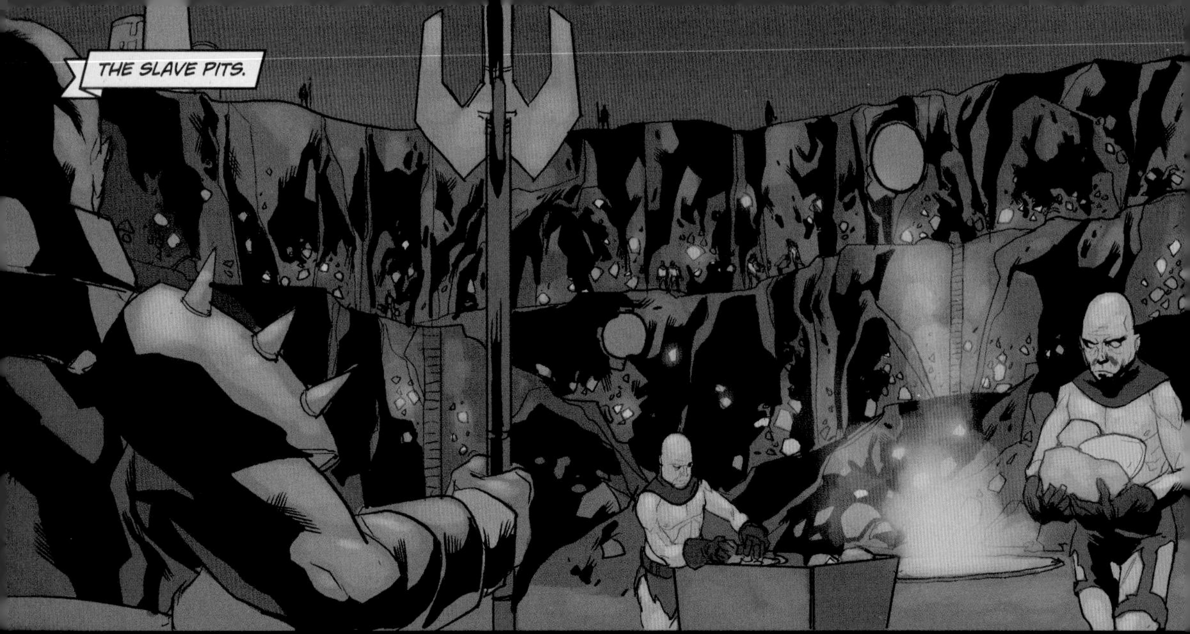
THE SLAVE PITS.

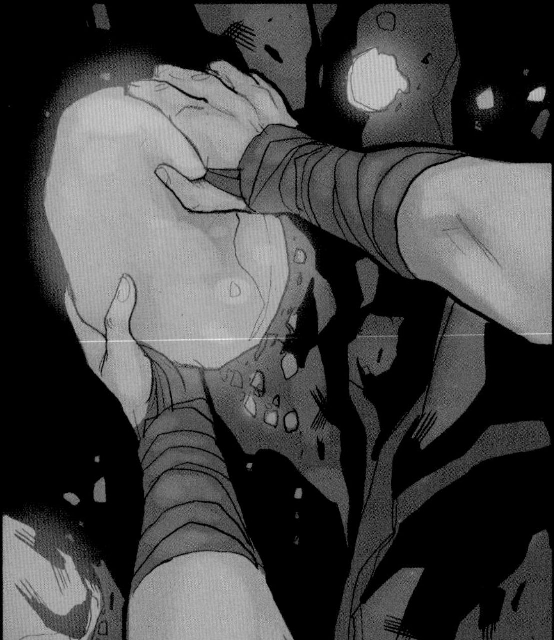

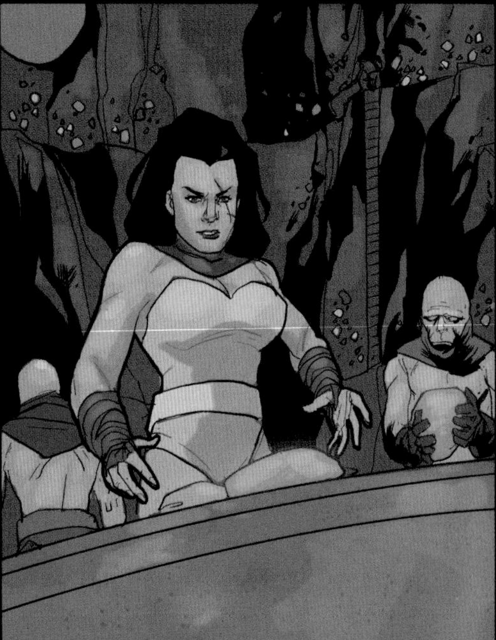

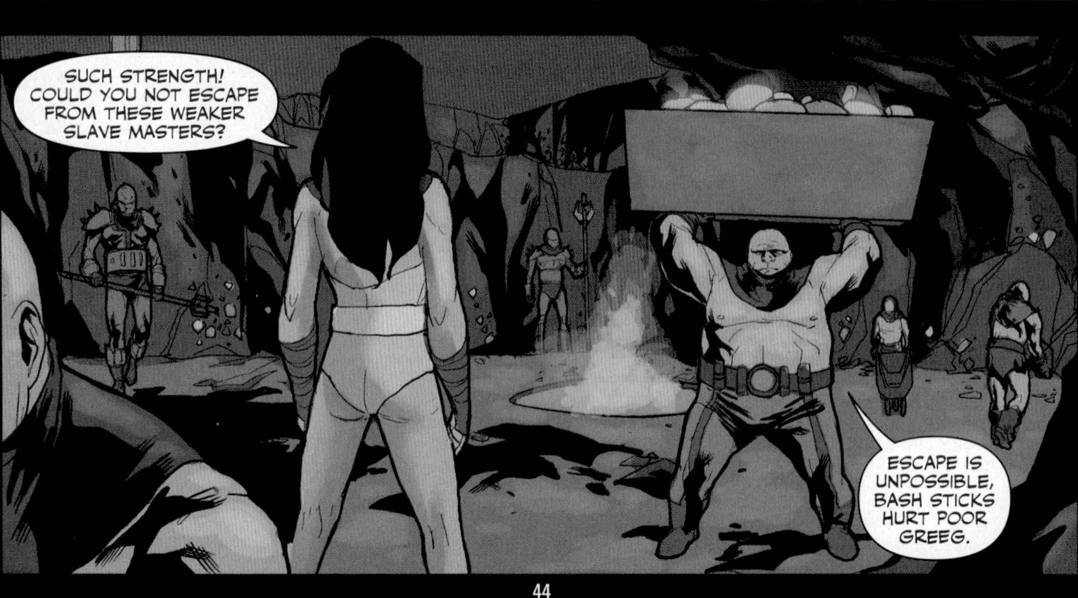
SUCH STRENGTH! COULD YOU NOT ESCAPE FROM THESE WEAKER SLAVE MASTERS?
ESCAPE IS UNPOSSIBLE, BASH STICKS HURT POOR GREEG.

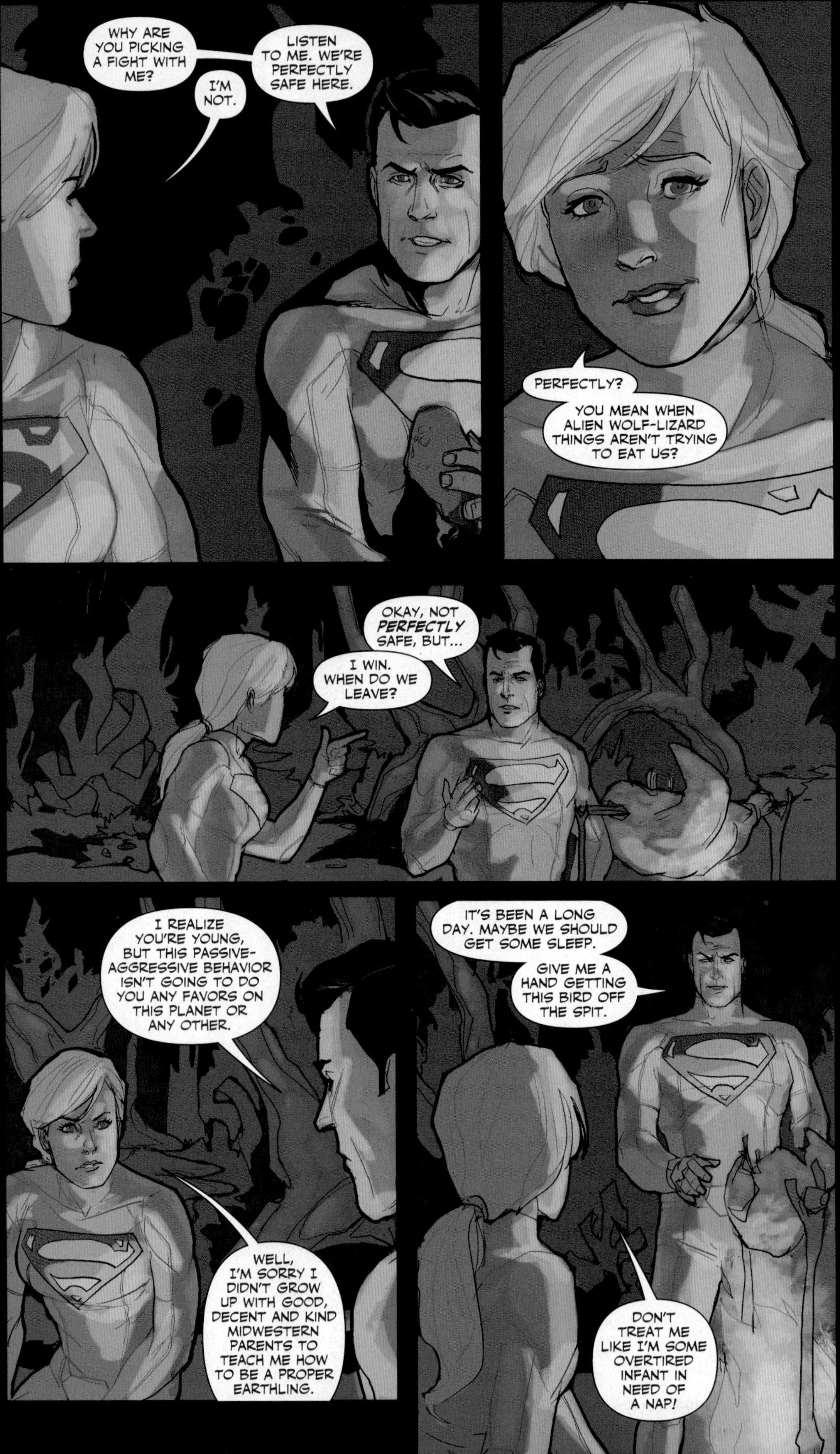
WHY ARE YOU PICKING A FIGHT WITH ME?
I'M NOT.
LISTEN TO ME. WE'RE PERFECTLY SAFE HERE.
PERFECTLY?
YOU MEAN WHEN ALIEN WOLF-LIZARD THINGS AREN'T TRYING TO EAT US?
OKAY, NOT *PERFECTLY* SAFE, BUT...
I WIN. WHEN DO WE LEAVE?
I REALIZE YOU'RE YOUNG, BUT THIS PASSIVE-AGGRESSIVE BEHAVIOR ISN'T GOING TO DO YOU ANY FAVORS ON THIS PLANET OR ANY OTHER.
WELL, I'M SORRY I DIDN'T GROW UP WITH GOOD, DECENT AND KIND MIDWESTERN PARENTS TO TEACH ME HOW TO BE A PROPER EARTHLING.
IT'S BEEN A LONG DAY. MAYBE WE SHOULD GET SOME SLEEP.
GIVE ME A HAND GETTING THIS BIRD OFF THE SPIT.
DON'T TREAT ME LIKE I'M SOME OVERTIRED INFANT IN NEED OF A NAP!

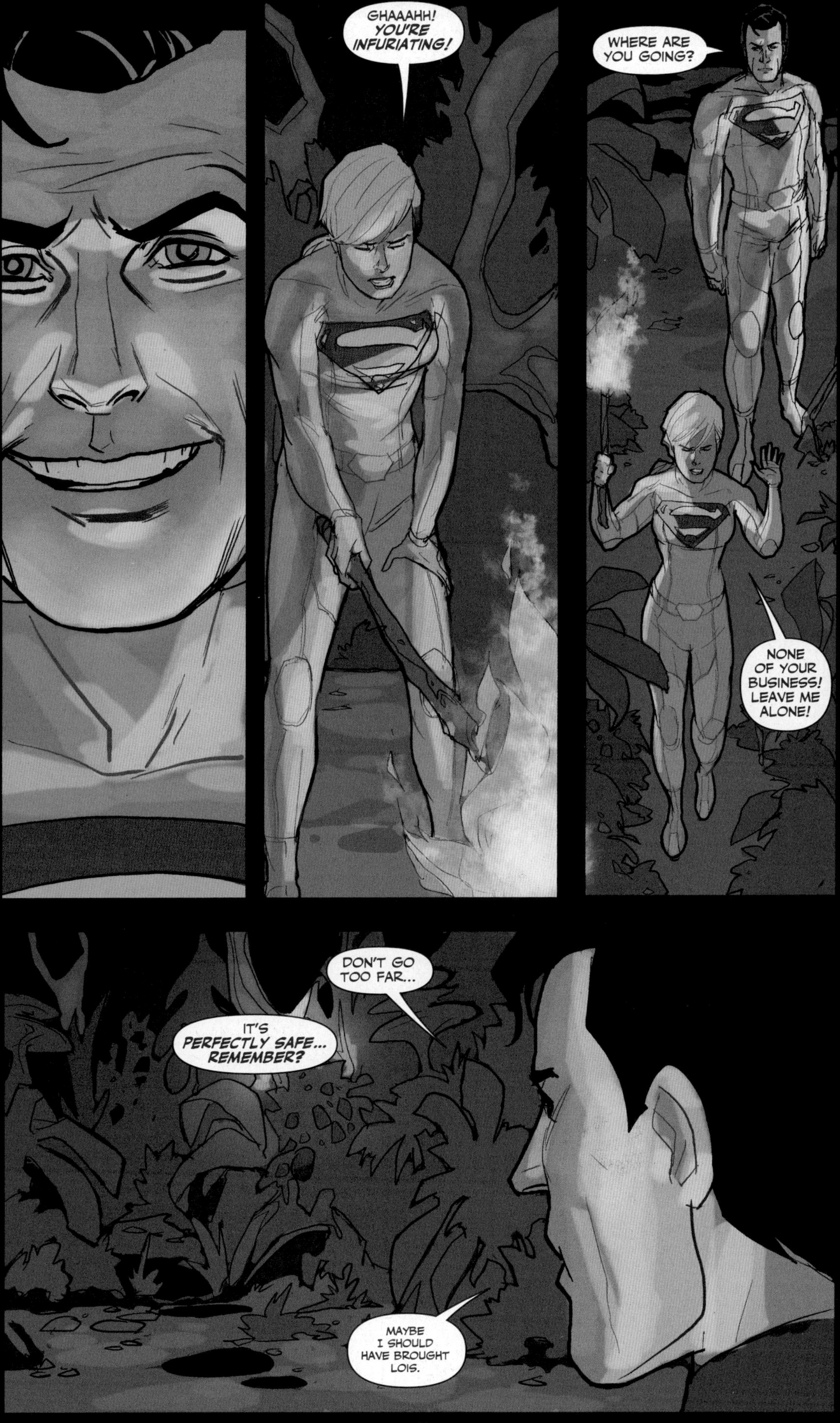
GHAAAHH! YOU'RE INFURIATING!
WHERE ARE YOU GOING?
NONE OF YOUR BUSINESS! LEAVE ME ALONE!
IT'S PERFECTLY SAFE... REMEMBER?
DON'T GO TOO FAR...
MAYBE I SHOULD HAVE BROUGHT LOIS.

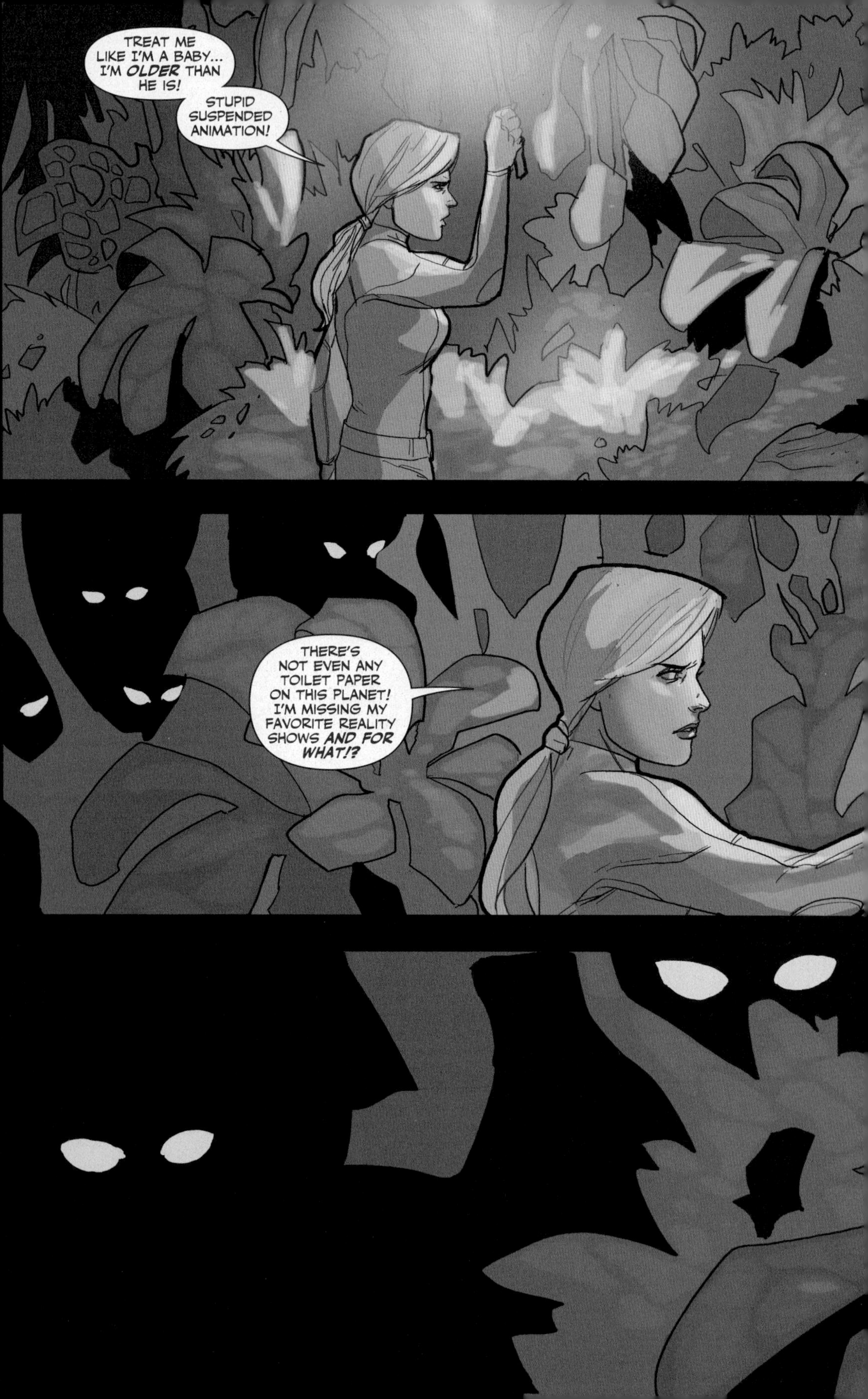

TREAT ME LIKE I'M A BABY... I'M *OLDER* THAN HE IS!
STUPID SUSPENDED ANIMATION!
THERE'S NOT EVEN ANY TOILET PAPER ON THIS PLANET! I'M MISSING MY FAVORITE REALITY SHOWS *AND FOR WHAT!?*

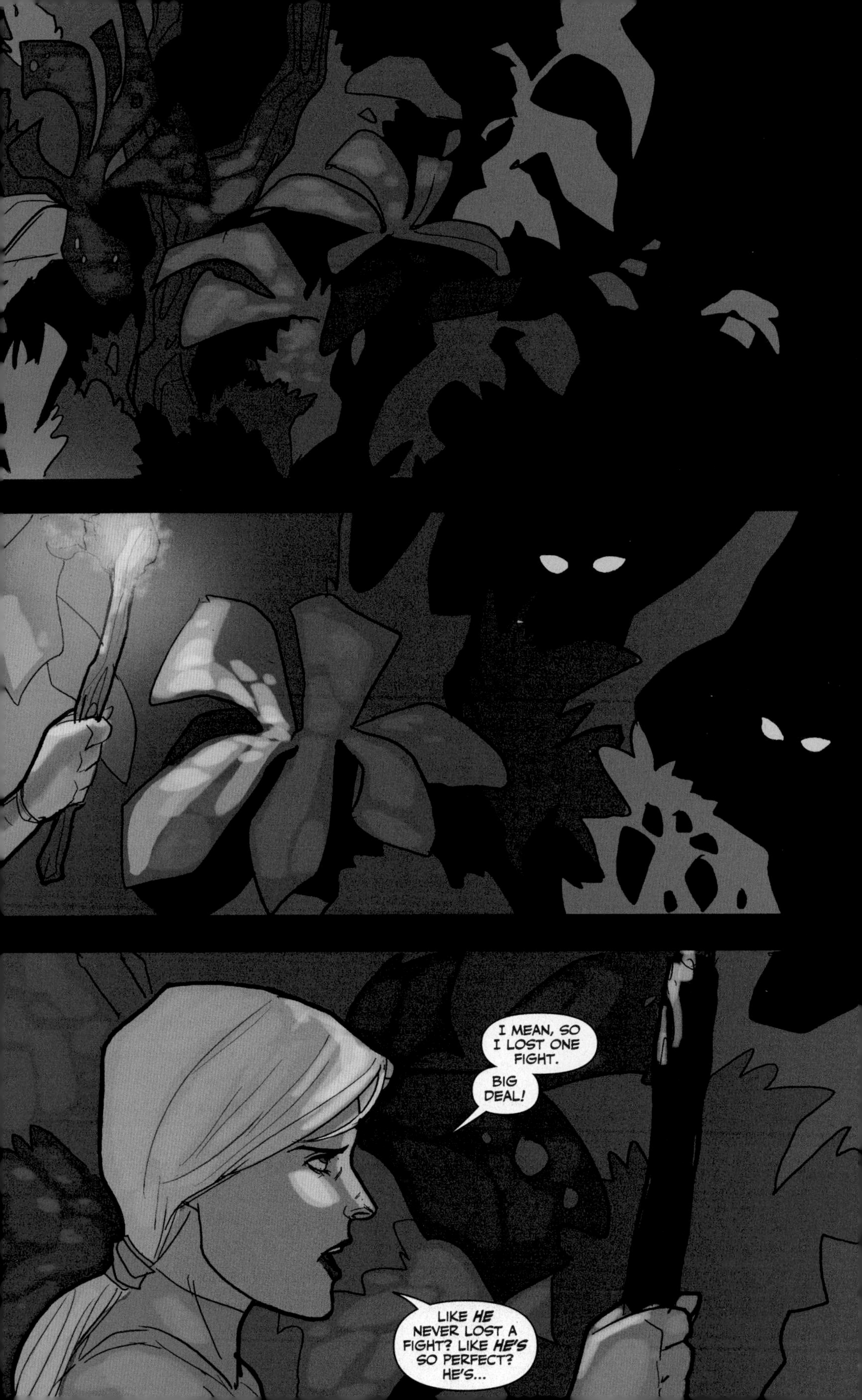
I MEAN, SO I LOST ONE FIGHT.
BIG DEAL!
LIKE *HE* NEVER LOST A FIGHT? LIKE *HE'S* SO PERFECT? HE'S...

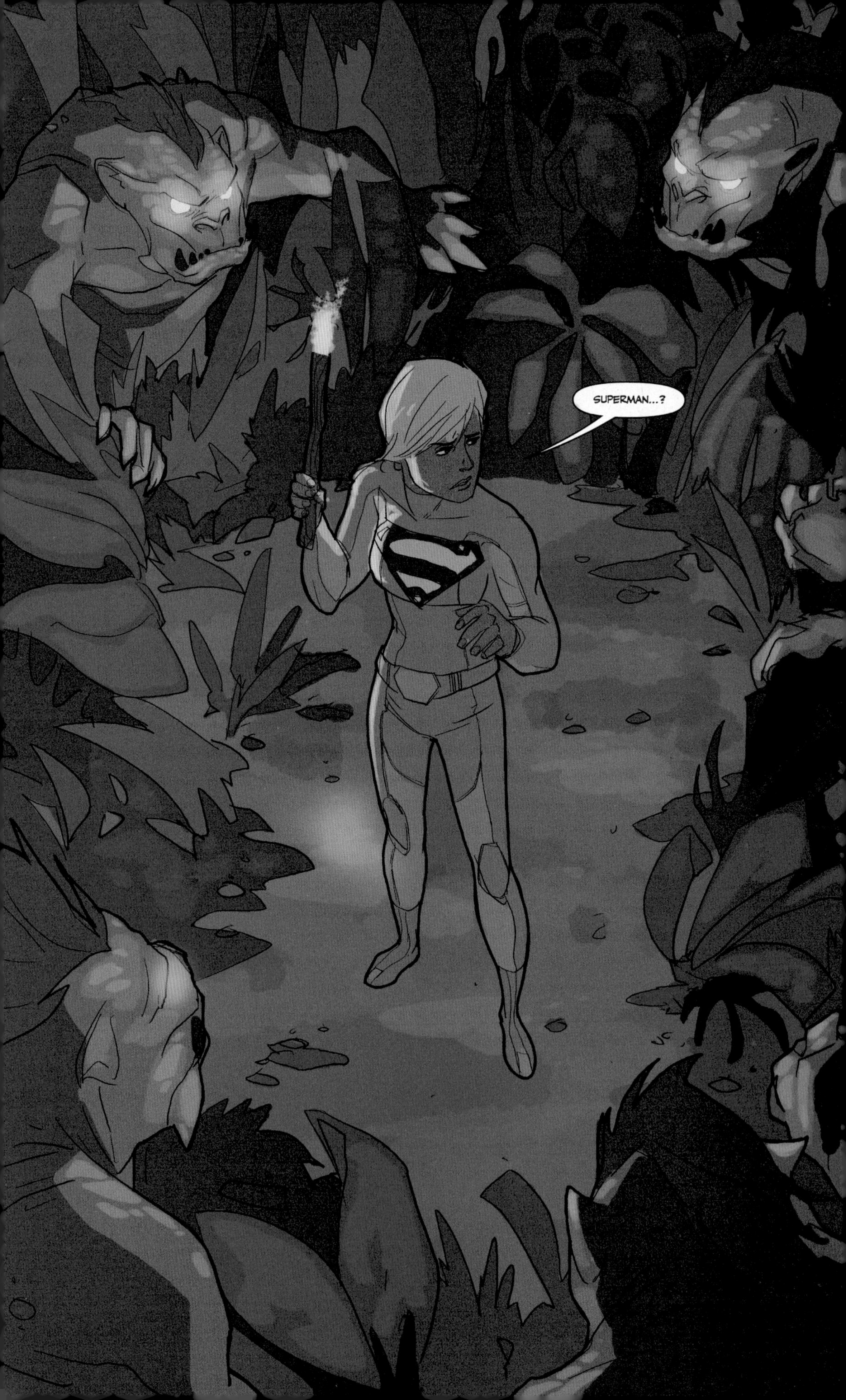
SUPERMAN...?

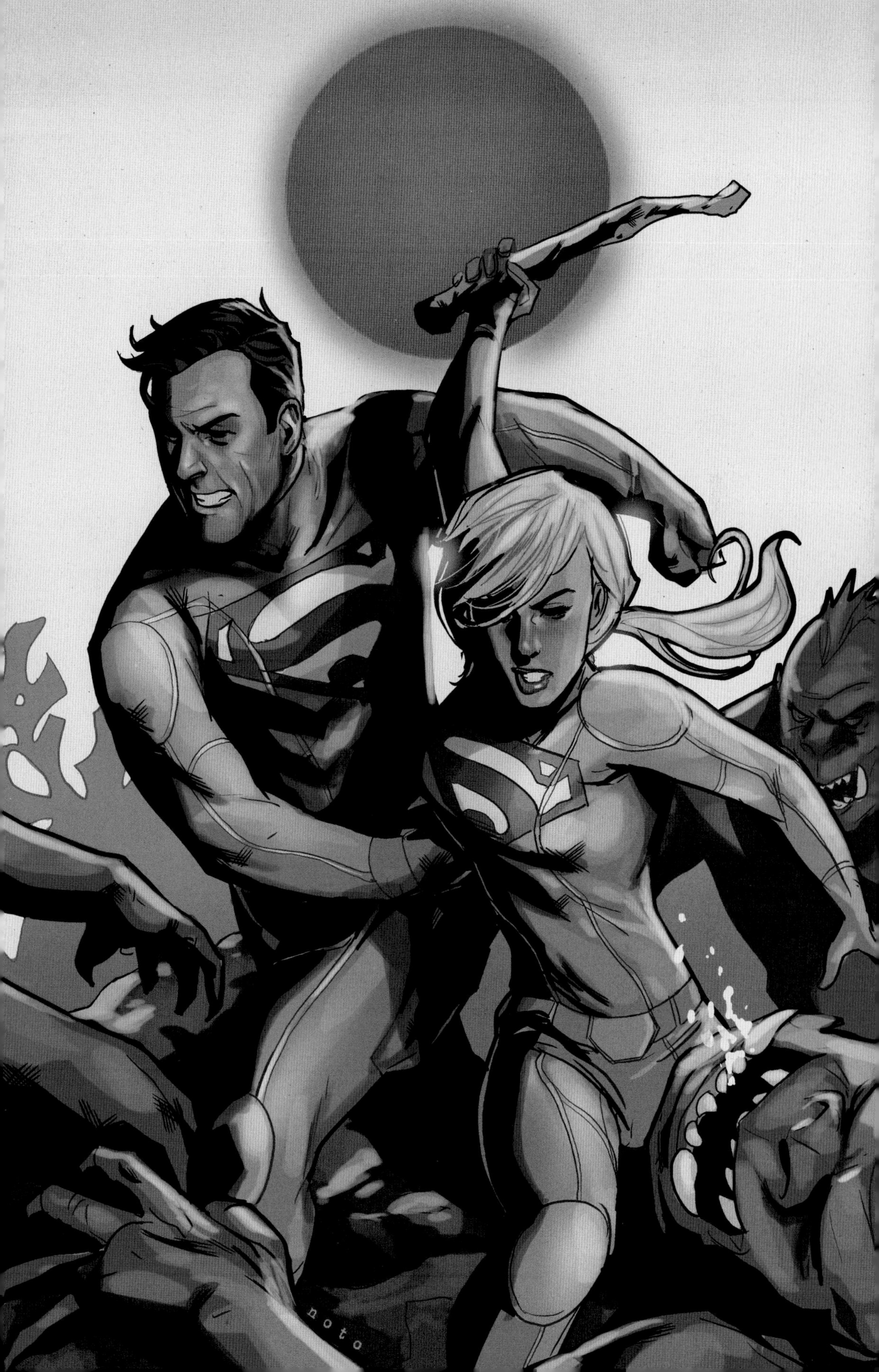
noto

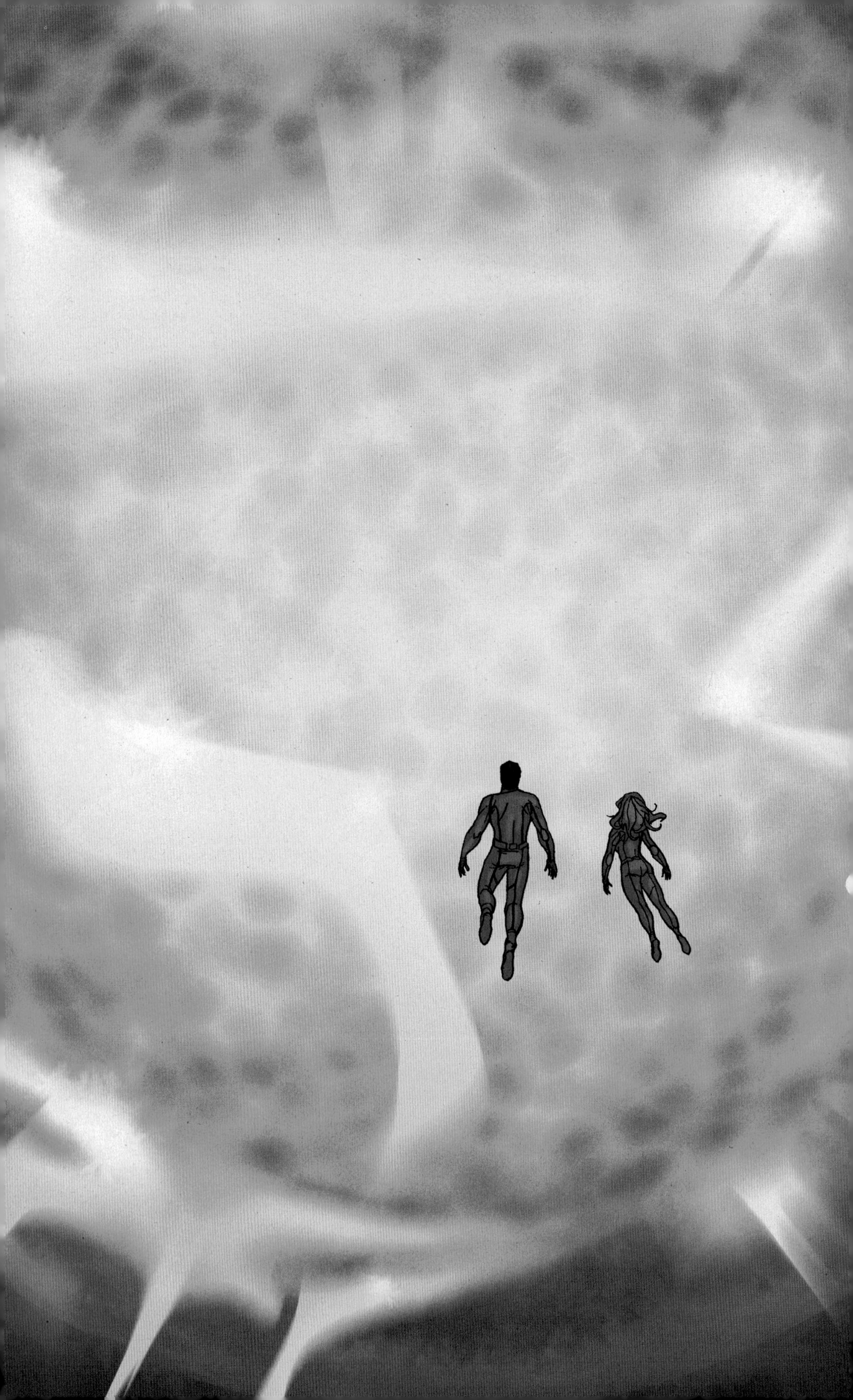

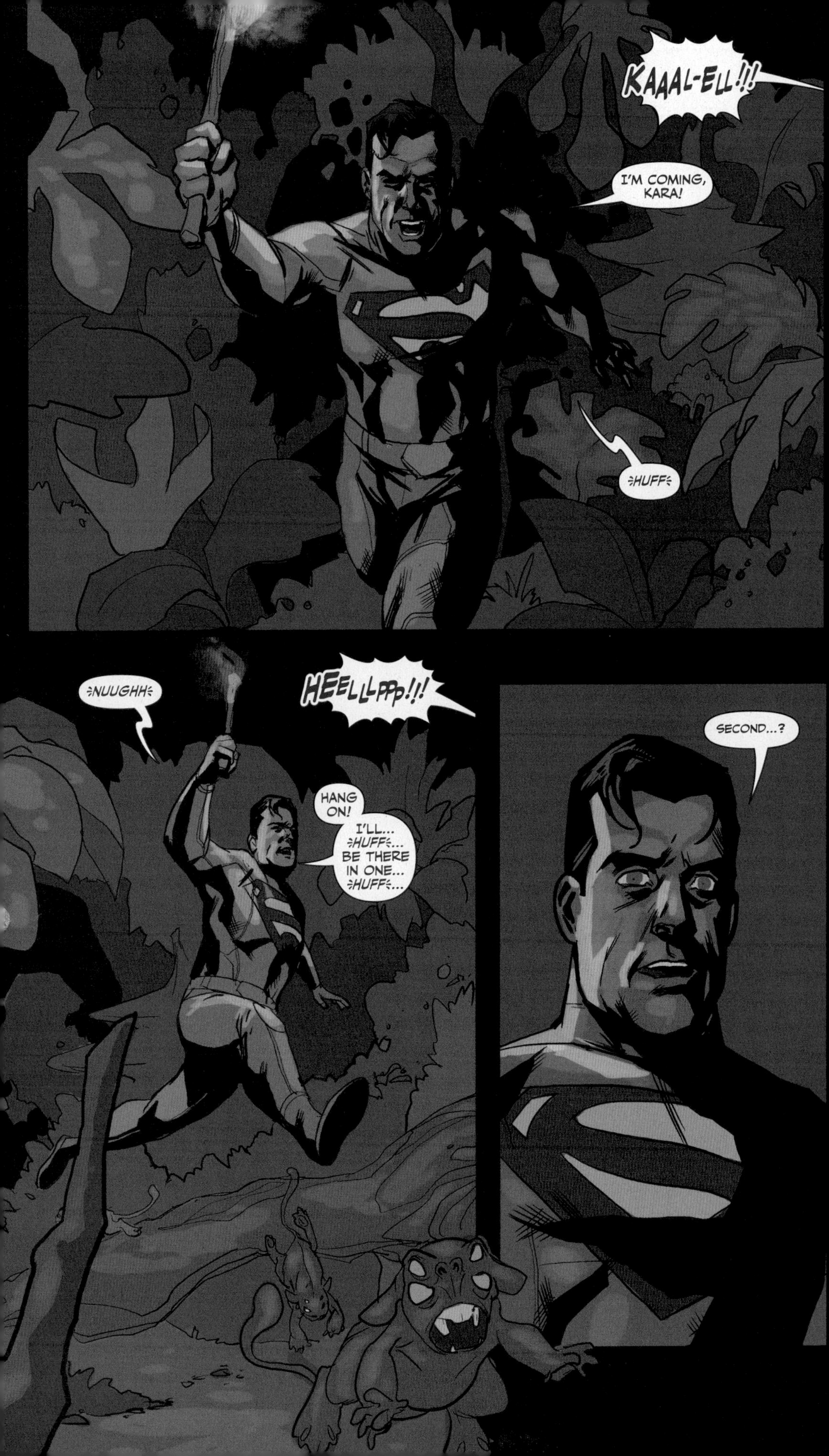
KAAAL-ELL!!!
I'M COMING, KARA!
HUFF
NUUGHH
HEELLLPPP!!!
HANG ON!
I'LL... HUFF... BE THERE IN ONE... HUFF...
SECOND...?

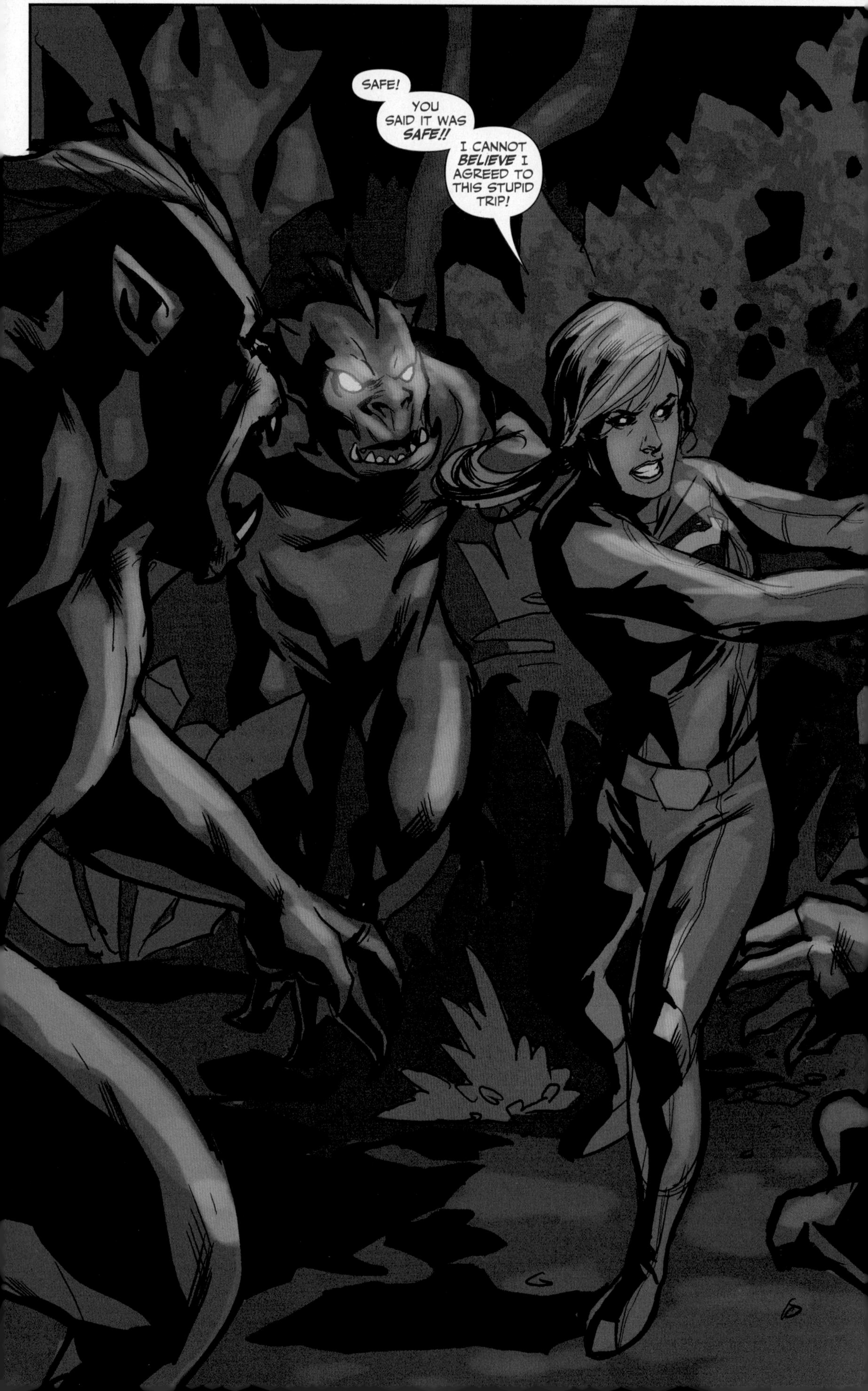
SAFE!
YOU SAID IT WAS SAFE!!
I CANNOT BELIEVE I AGREED TO THIS STUPID TRIP!

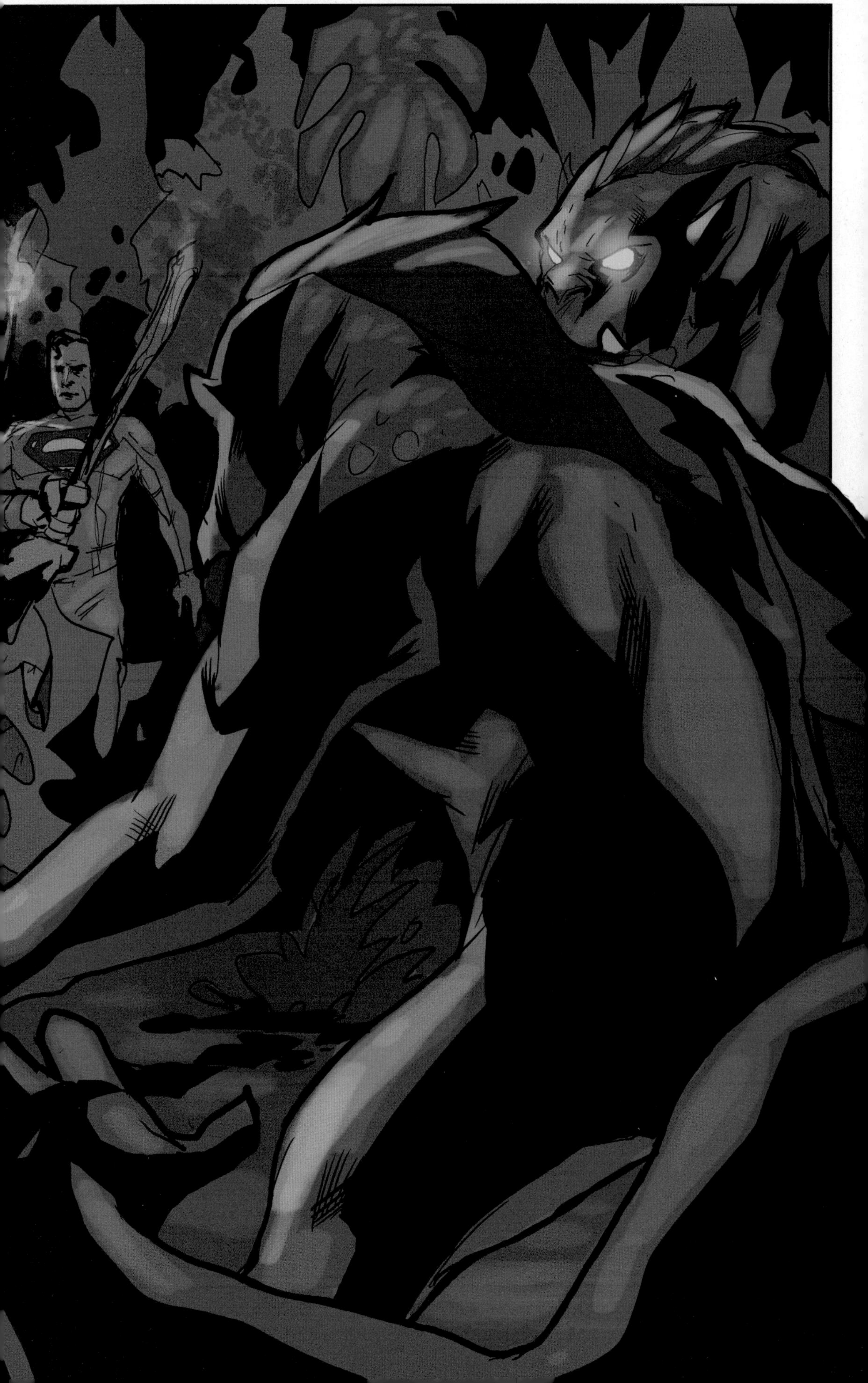

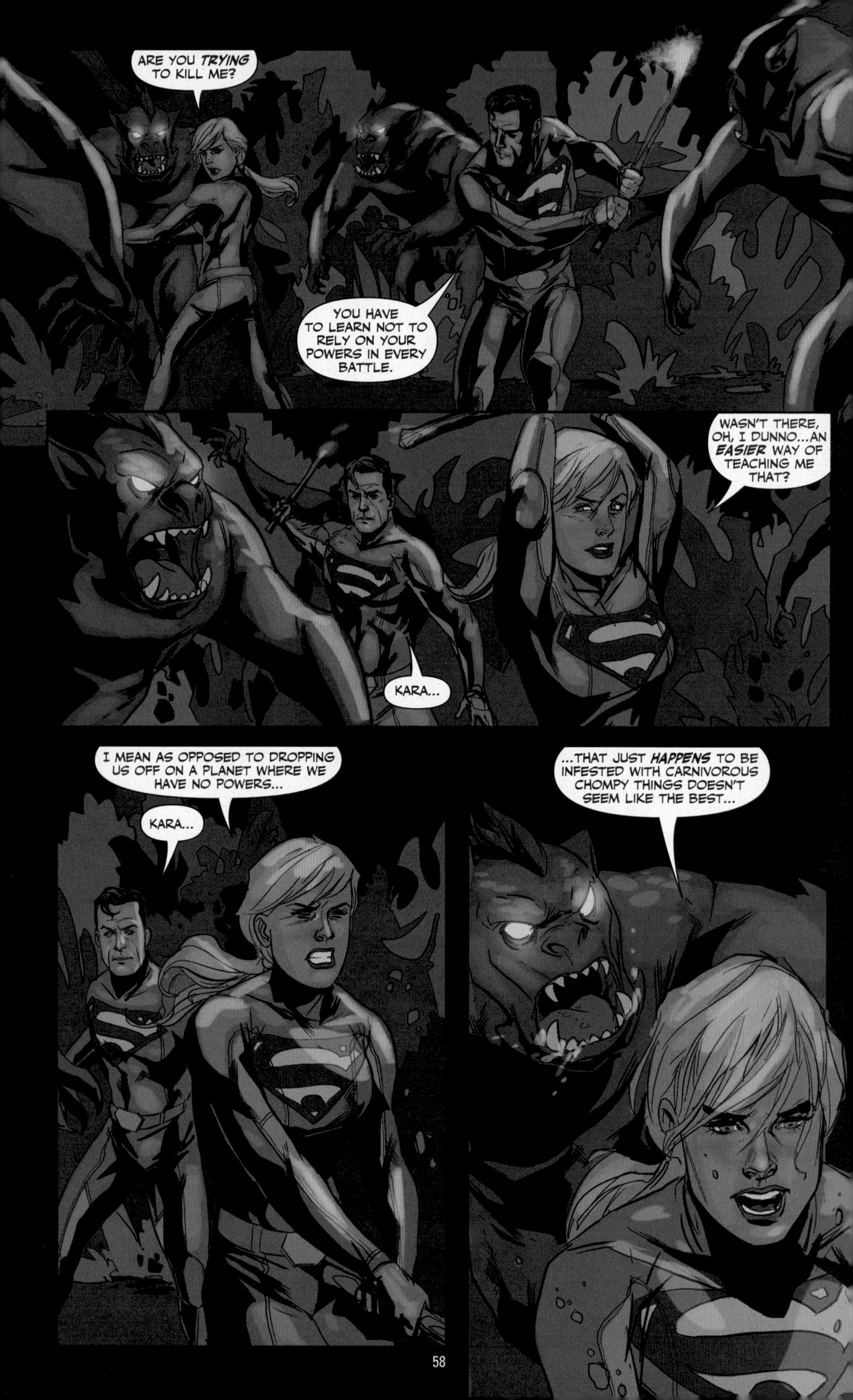
ARE YOU TRYING TO KILL ME?
YOU HAVE TO LEARN NOT TO RELY ON YOUR POWERS IN EVERY BATTLE.
WASN'T THERE, OH, I DUNNO...AN EASIER WAY OF TEACHING ME THAT?
KARA...
I MEAN AS OPPOSED TO DROPPING US OFF ON A PLANET WHERE WE HAVE NO POWERS...
KARA...
...THAT JUST HAPPENS TO BE INFESTED WITH CARNIVOROUS CHOMPY THINGS DOESN'T SEEM LIKE THE BEST...

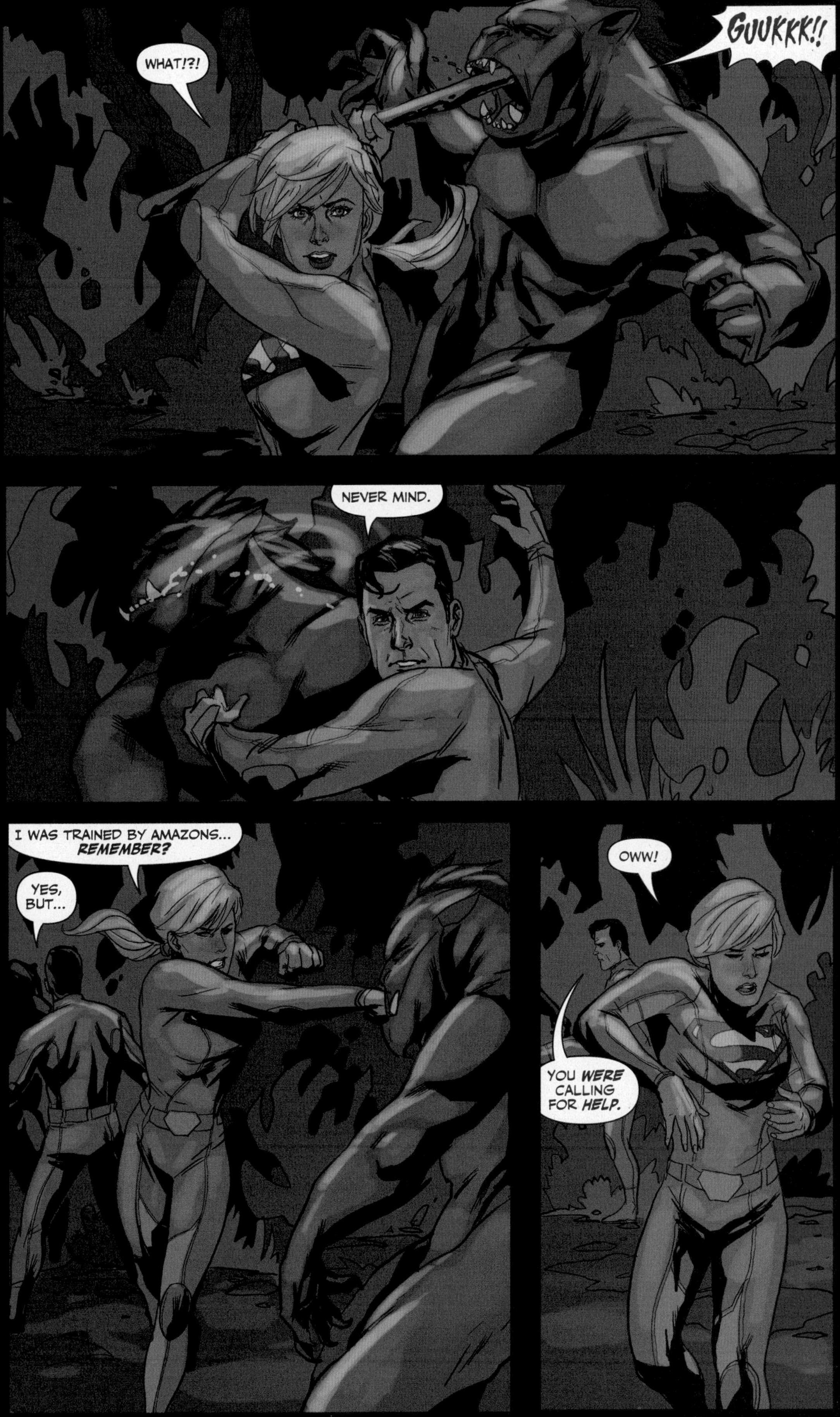
WHAT!?!
GUUKKK!!
NEVER MIND.
I WAS TRAINED BY AMAZONS... REMEMBER?
YES, BUT...
OWW!
YOU WERE CALLING FOR HELP.

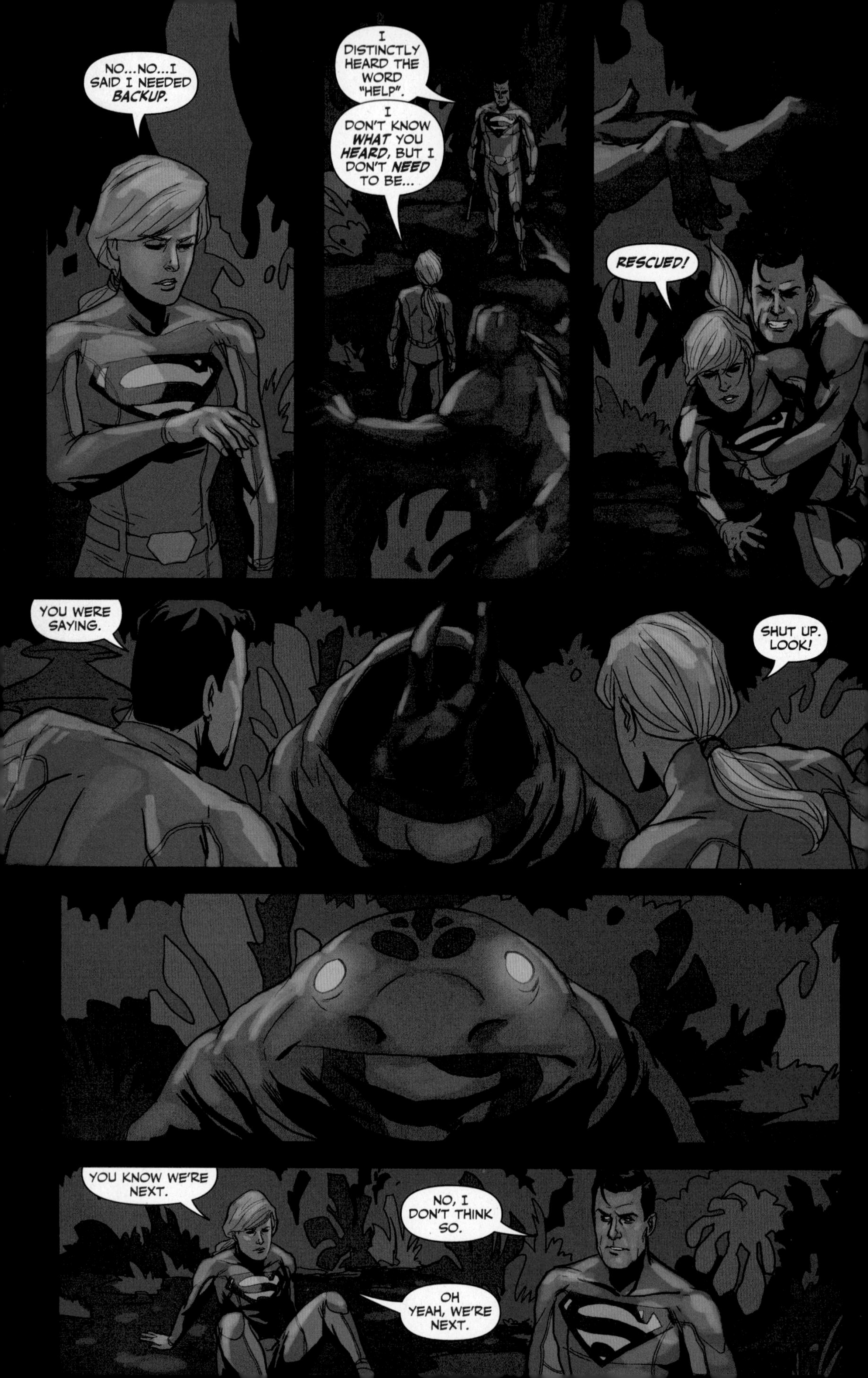
NO...NO...I SAID I NEEDED *BACKUP.*
I DISTINCTLY HEARD THE WORD "HELP".
I DON'T KNOW *WHAT* YOU *HEARD,* BUT I DON'T *NEED* TO BE...
RESCUED!
YOU WERE SAYING.
SHUT UP. LOOK!
YOU KNOW WE'RE NEXT.
NO, I DON'T THINK SO.
OH YEAH, WE'RE NEXT.

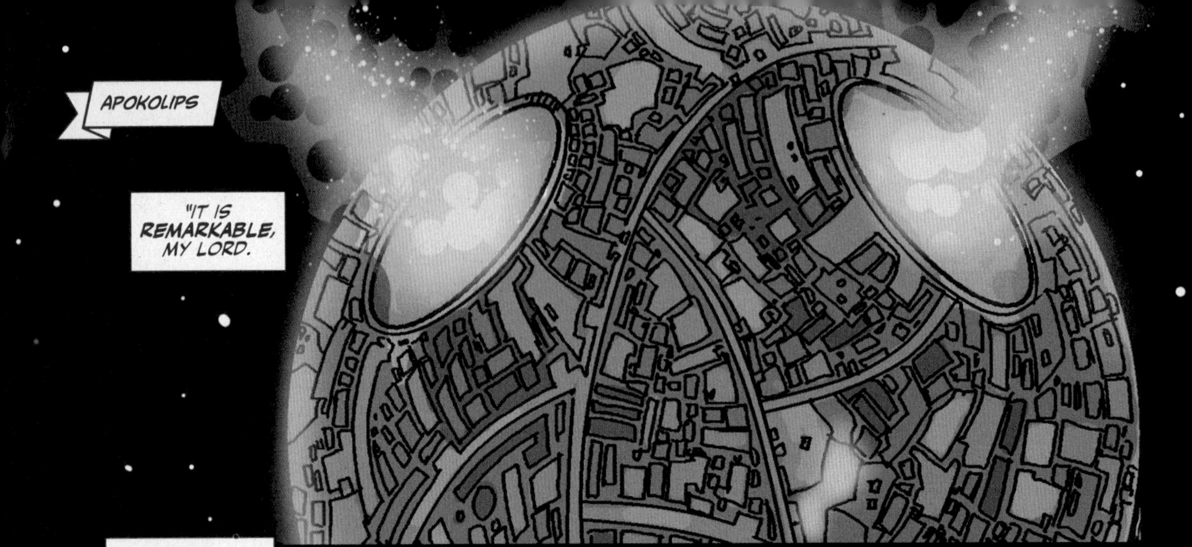
APOKOLIPS
"IT IS REMARKABLE, MY LORD.

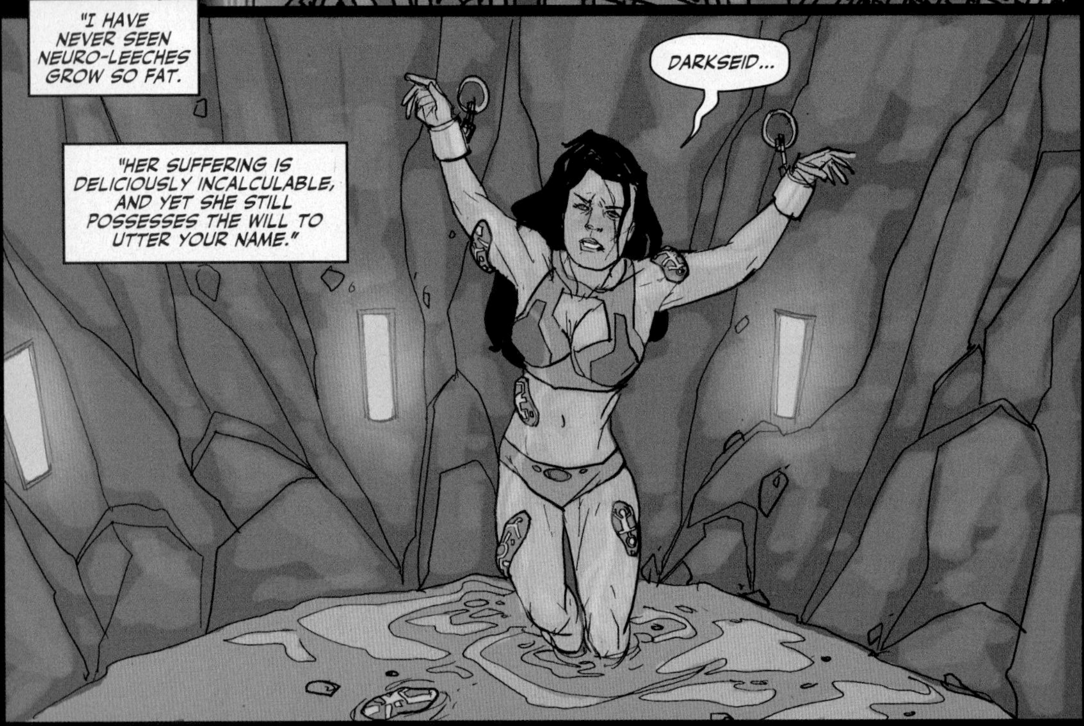
"I HAVE NEVER SEEN NEURO-LEECHES GROW SO FAT.
DARKSEID...
"HER SUFFERING IS DELICIOUSLY INCALCULABLE, AND YET SHE STILL POSSESSES THE WILL TO UTTER YOUR NAME."

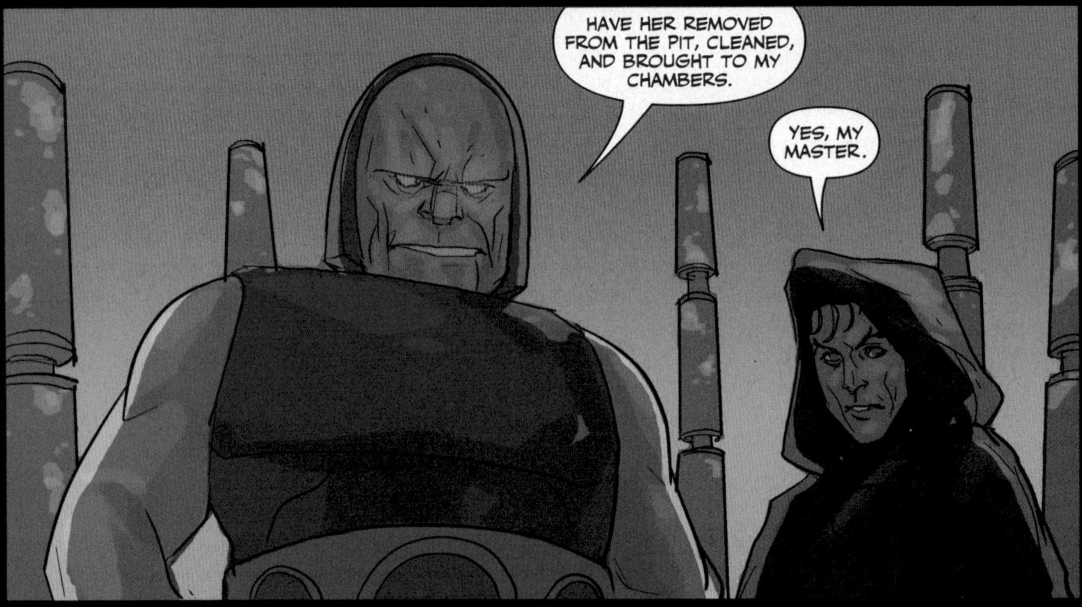
HAVE HER REMOVED FROM THE PIT, CLEANED, AND BROUGHT TO MY CHAMBERS.
YES, MY MASTER.

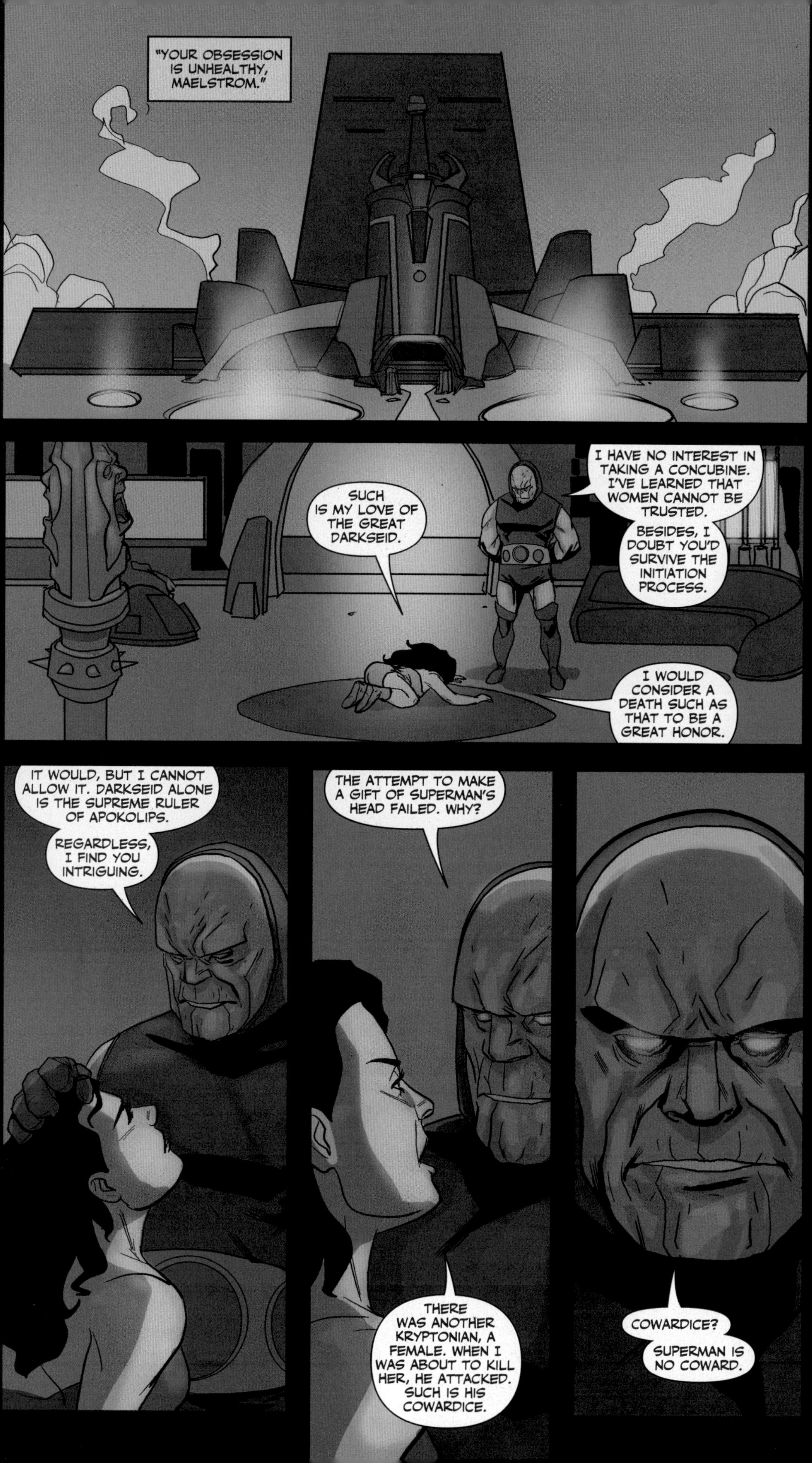
"YOUR OBSESSION IS UNHEALTHY, MAELSTROM."
SUCH IS MY LOVE OF THE GREAT DARKSEID.
I HAVE NO INTEREST IN TAKING A CONCUBINE. I'VE LEARNED THAT WOMEN CANNOT BE TRUSTED.
BESIDES, I DOUBT YOU'D SURVIVE THE INITIATION PROCESS.
I WOULD CONSIDER A DEATH SUCH AS THAT TO BE A GREAT HONOR.
IT WOULD, BUT I CANNOT ALLOW IT. DARKSEID ALONE IS THE SUPREME RULER OF APOKOLIPS.
REGARDLESS, I FIND YOU INTRIGUING.
THE ATTEMPT TO MAKE A GIFT OF SUPERMAN'S HEAD FAILED. WHY?
THERE WAS ANOTHER KRYPTONIAN, A FEMALE. WHEN I WAS ABOUT TO KILL HER, HE ATTACKED. SUCH IS HIS COWARDICE.
COWARDICE?
SUPERMAN IS NO COWARD.

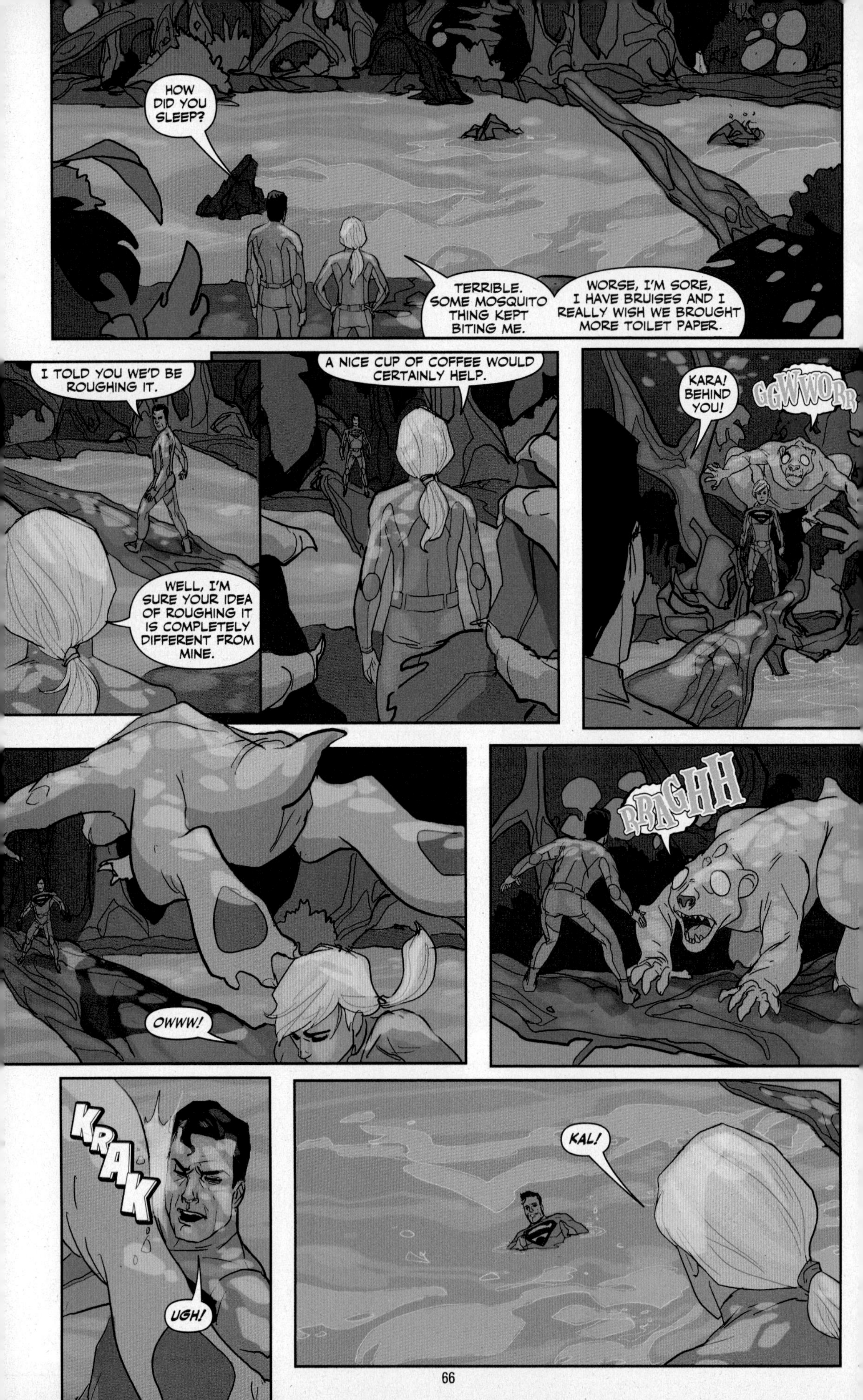
HOW DID YOU SLEEP?
TERRIBLE. SOME MOSQUITO THING KEPT BITING ME.
WORSE, I'M SORE, I HAVE BRUISES AND I REALLY WISH WE BROUGHT MORE TOILET PAPER.
I TOLD YOU WE'D BE ROUGHING IT.
WELL, I'M SURE YOUR IDEA OF ROUGHING IT IS COMPLETELY DIFFERENT FROM MINE.
A NICE CUP OF COFFEE WOULD CERTAINLY HELP.
KARA! BEHIND YOU!
GGWWORR
OWWW!
RRAGHH
KRAK
UGH!
KAL!

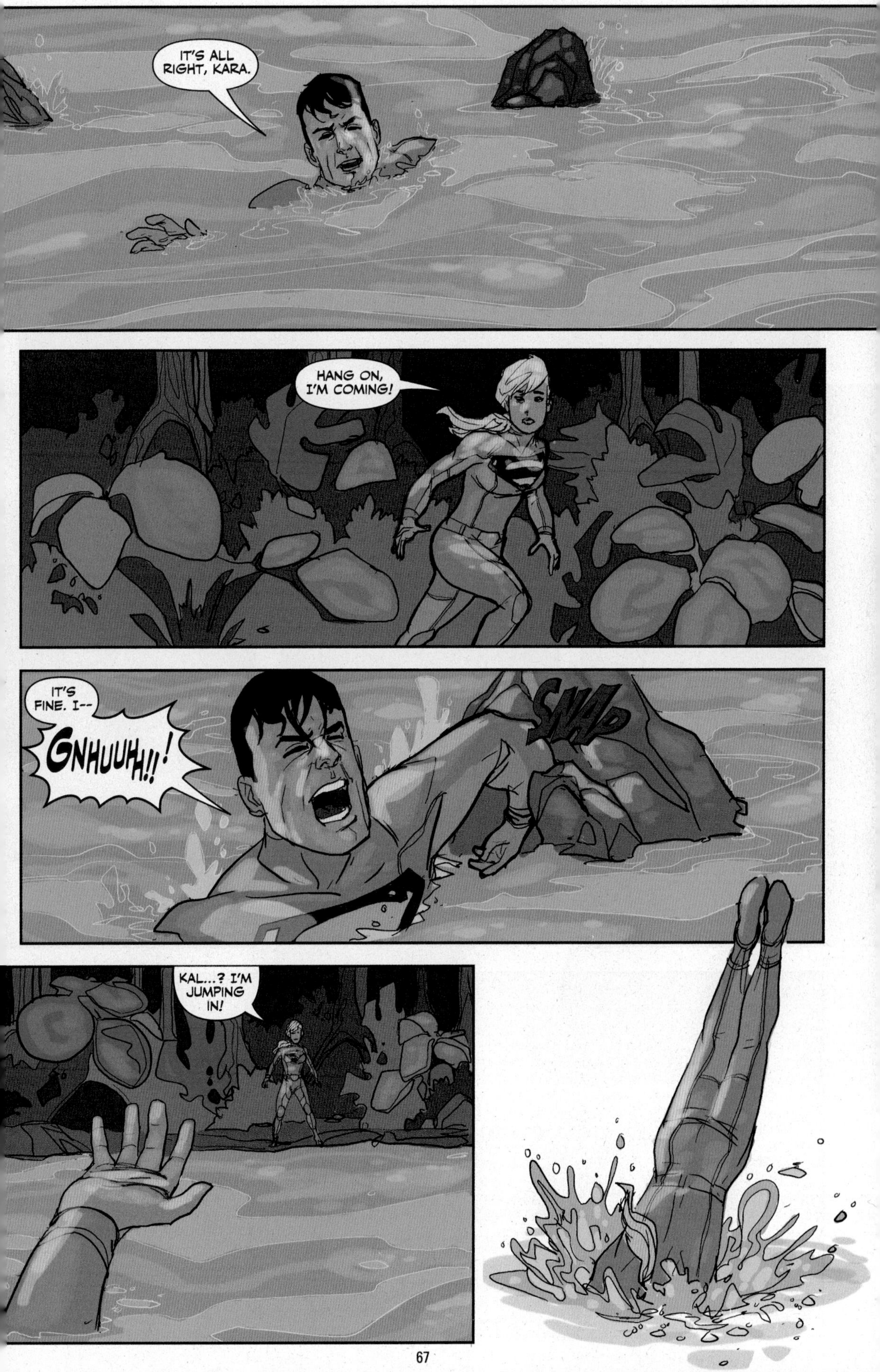
IT'S ALL RIGHT, KARA.
HANG ON, I'M COMING!
IT'S FINE. I--
GNHUUHH!!!
SNAP
KAL...? I'M JUMPING IN!

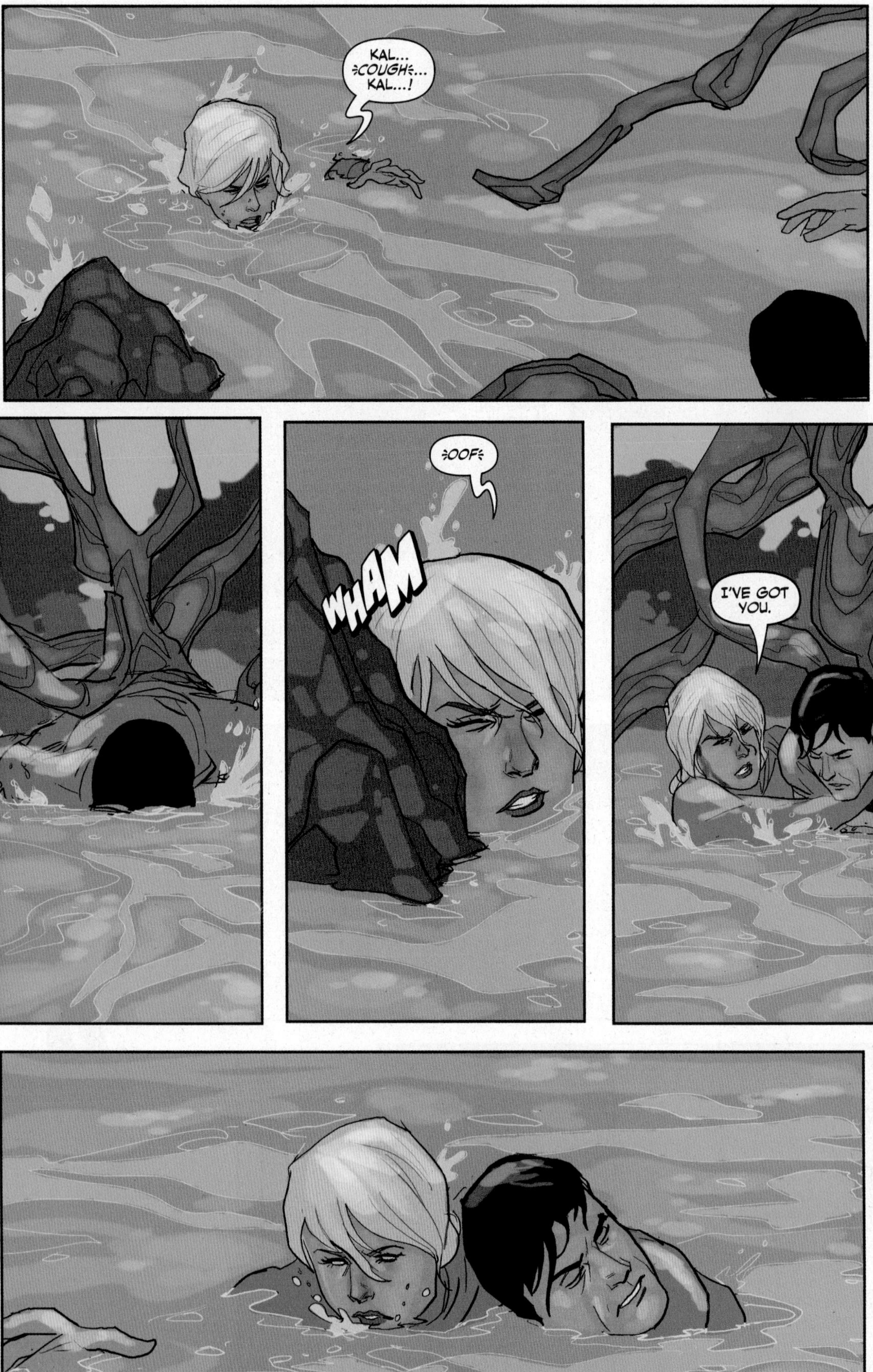
KAL... COUGH... KAL...!
OOF
WHAM
I'VE GOT YOU.

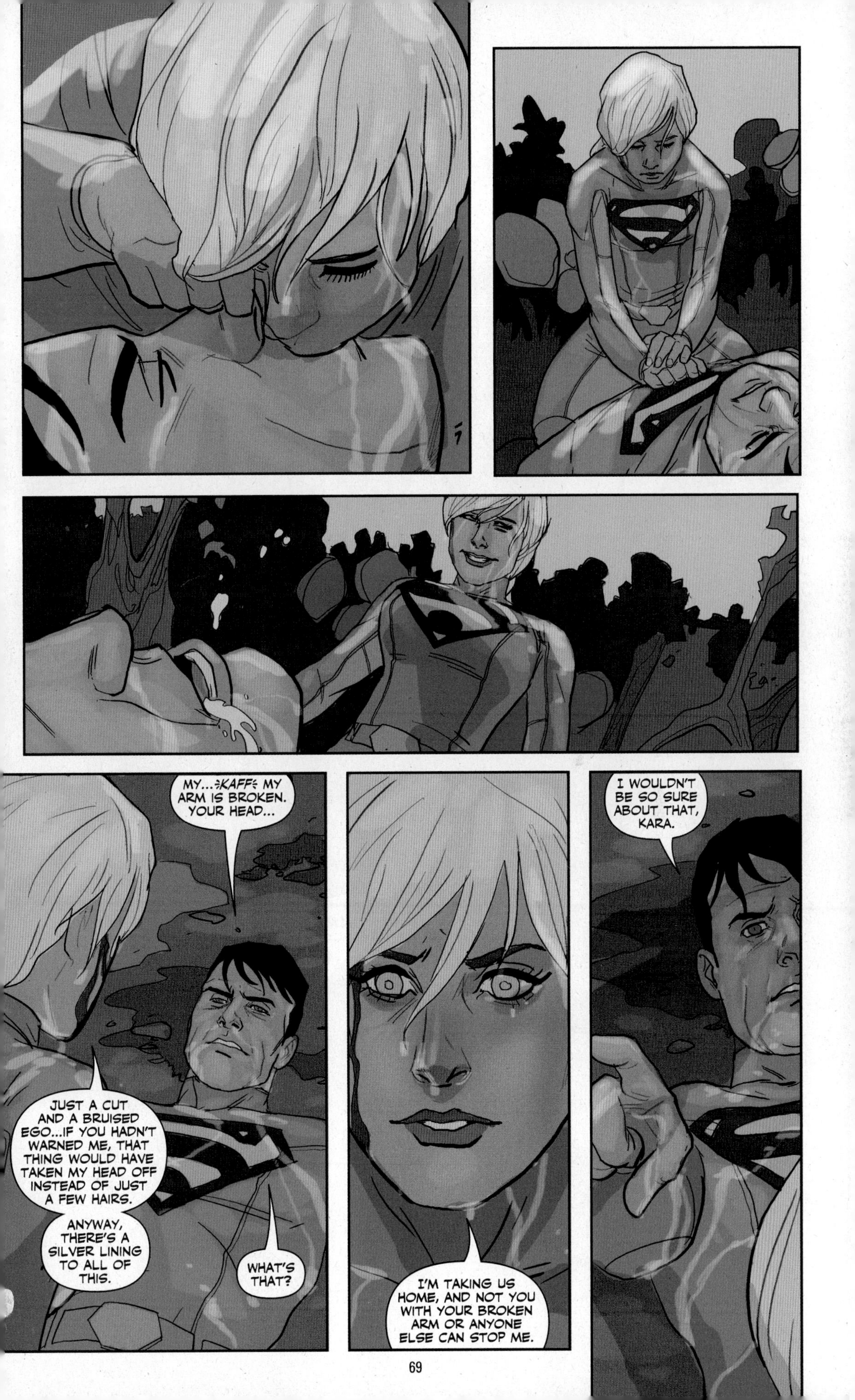
MY...⁜KAFF⁜ MY ARM IS BROKEN. YOUR HEAD...
JUST A CUT AND A BRUISED EGO...IF YOU HADN'T WARNED ME, THAT THING WOULD HAVE TAKEN MY HEAD OFF INSTEAD OF JUST A FEW HAIRS.
ANYWAY, THERE'S A SILVER LINING TO ALL OF THIS.
WHAT'S THAT?
I'M TAKING US HOME, AND NOT YOU WITH YOUR BROKEN ARM OR ANYONE ELSE CAN STOP ME.
I WOULDN'T BE SO SURE ABOUT THAT, KARA.

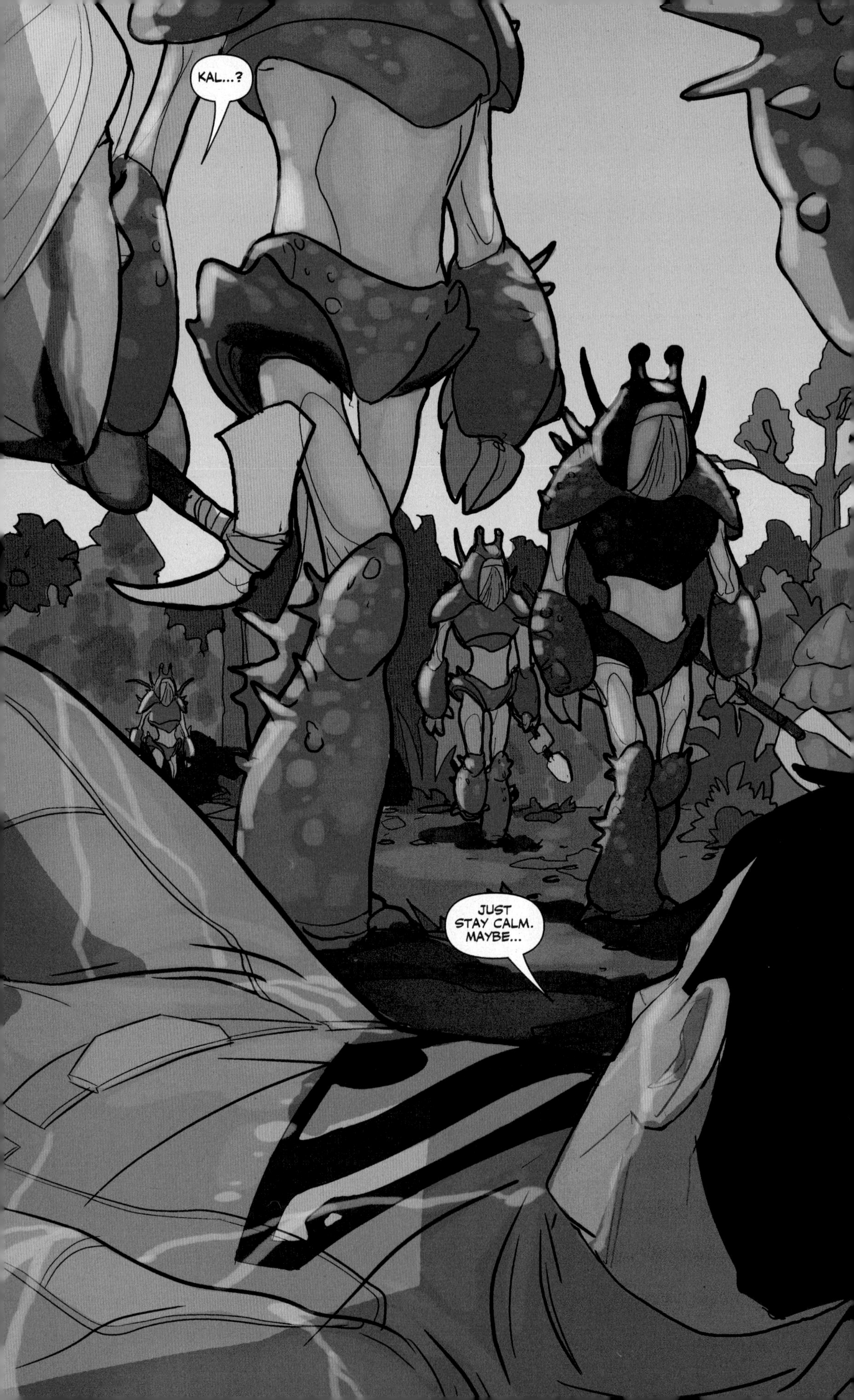
KAL...?
JUST STAY CALM. MAYBE...

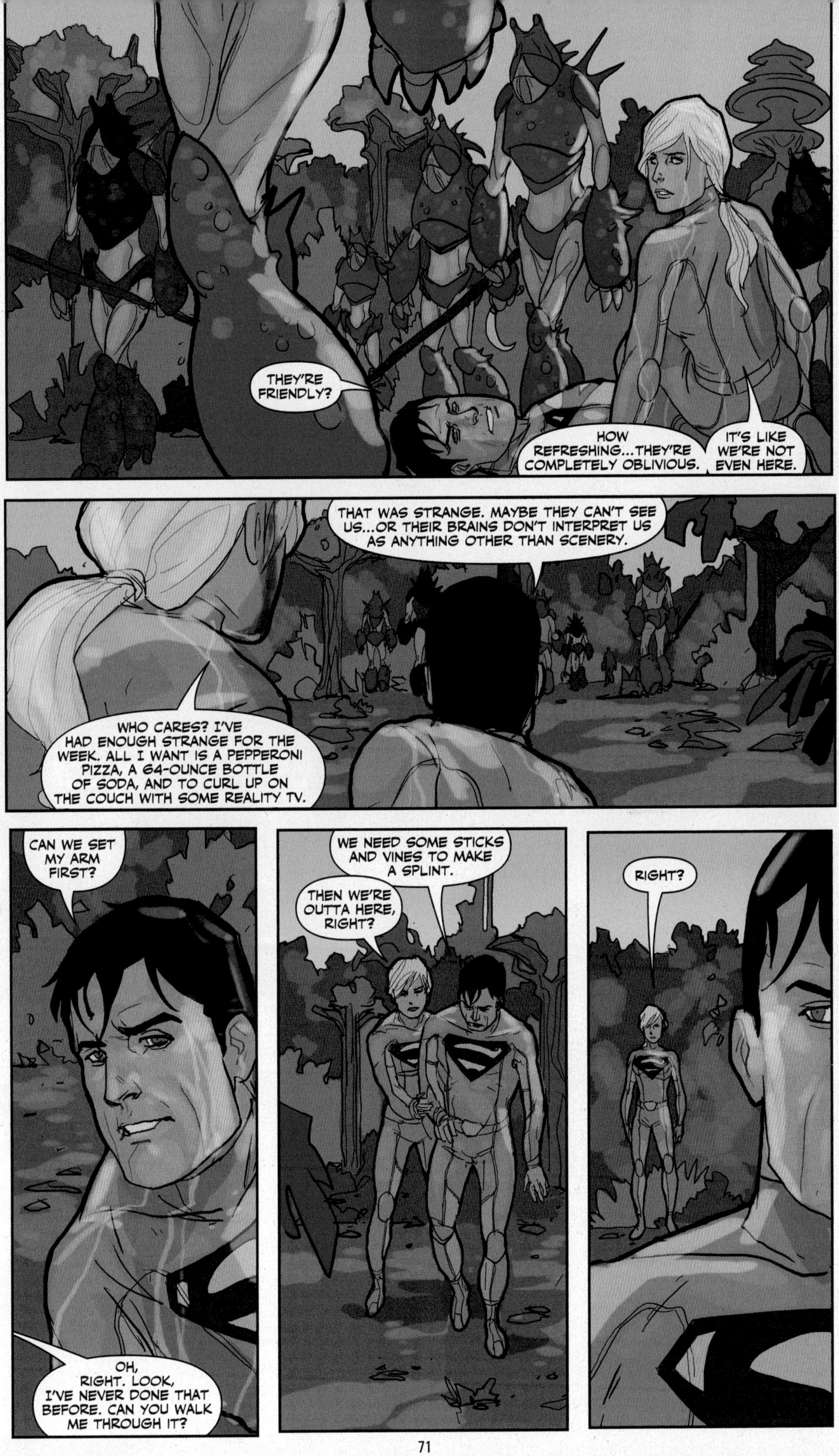
THEY'RE FRIENDLY?
HOW REFRESHING...THEY'RE COMPLETELY OBLIVIOUS.
IT'S LIKE WE'RE NOT EVEN HERE.
THAT WAS STRANGE. MAYBE THEY CAN'T SEE US...OR THEIR BRAINS DON'T INTERPRET US AS ANYTHING OTHER THAN SCENERY.
WHO CARES? I'VE HAD ENOUGH STRANGE FOR THE WEEK. ALL I WANT IS A PEPPERONI PIZZA, A 64-OUNCE BOTTLE OF SODA, AND TO CURL UP ON THE COUCH WITH SOME REALITY TV.
CAN WE SET MY ARM FIRST?
OH, RIGHT. LOOK, I'VE NEVER DONE THAT BEFORE. CAN YOU WALK ME THROUGH IT?
WE NEED SOME STICKS AND VINES TO MAKE A SPLINT.
THEN WE'RE OUTTA HERE, RIGHT?
RIGHT?

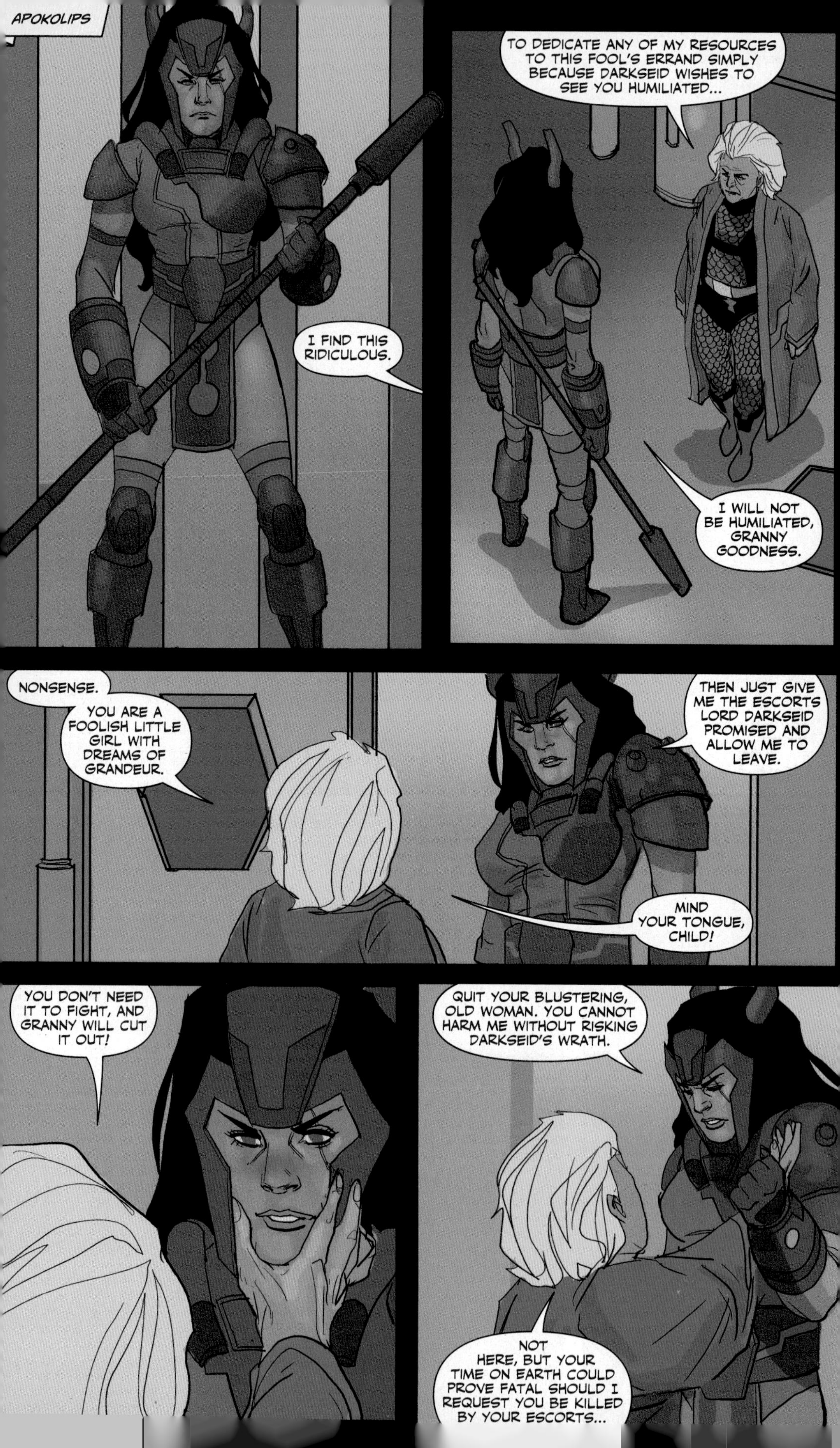
APOKOLIPS
I FIND THIS RIDICULOUS.
TO DEDICATE ANY OF MY RESOURCES TO THIS FOOL'S ERRAND SIMPLY BECAUSE DARKSEID WISHES TO SEE YOU HUMILIATED...
I WILL NOT BE HUMILIATED, GRANNY GOODNESS.
NONSENSE.
YOU ARE A FOOLISH LITTLE GIRL WITH DREAMS OF GRANDEUR.
THEN JUST GIVE ME THE ESCORTS LORD DARKSEID PROMISED AND ALLOW ME TO LEAVE.
MIND YOUR TONGUE, CHILD!
YOU DON'T NEED IT TO FIGHT, AND GRANNY WILL CUT IT OUT!
QUIT YOUR BLUSTERING, OLD WOMAN. YOU CANNOT HARM ME WITHOUT RISKING DARKSEID'S WRATH.
NOT HERE, BUT YOUR TIME ON EARTH COULD PROVE FATAL SHOULD I REQUEST YOU BE KILLED BY YOUR ESCORTS...

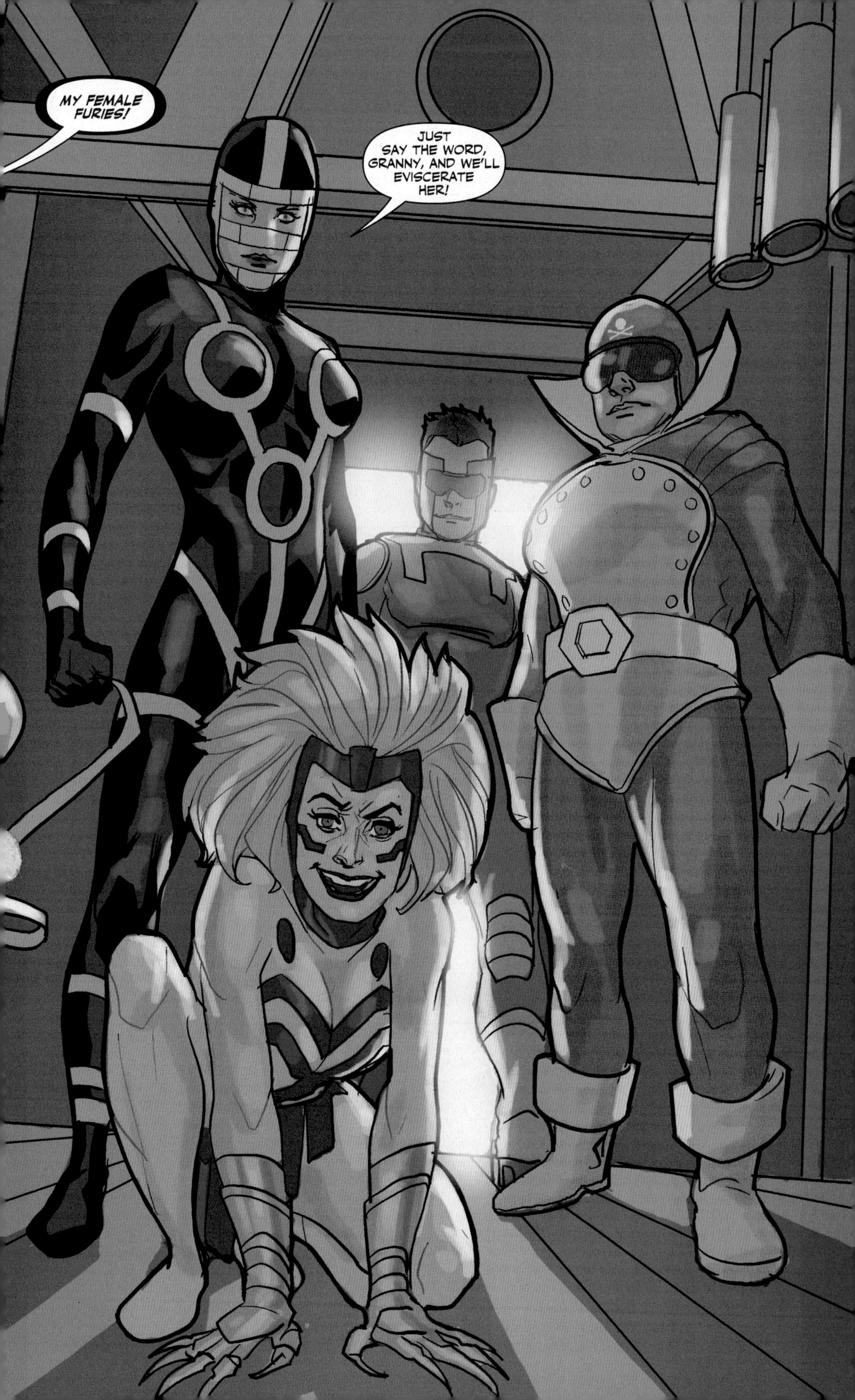
MY FEMALE FURIES!
JUST SAY THE WORD, GRANNY, AND WE'LL EVISCERATE HER!

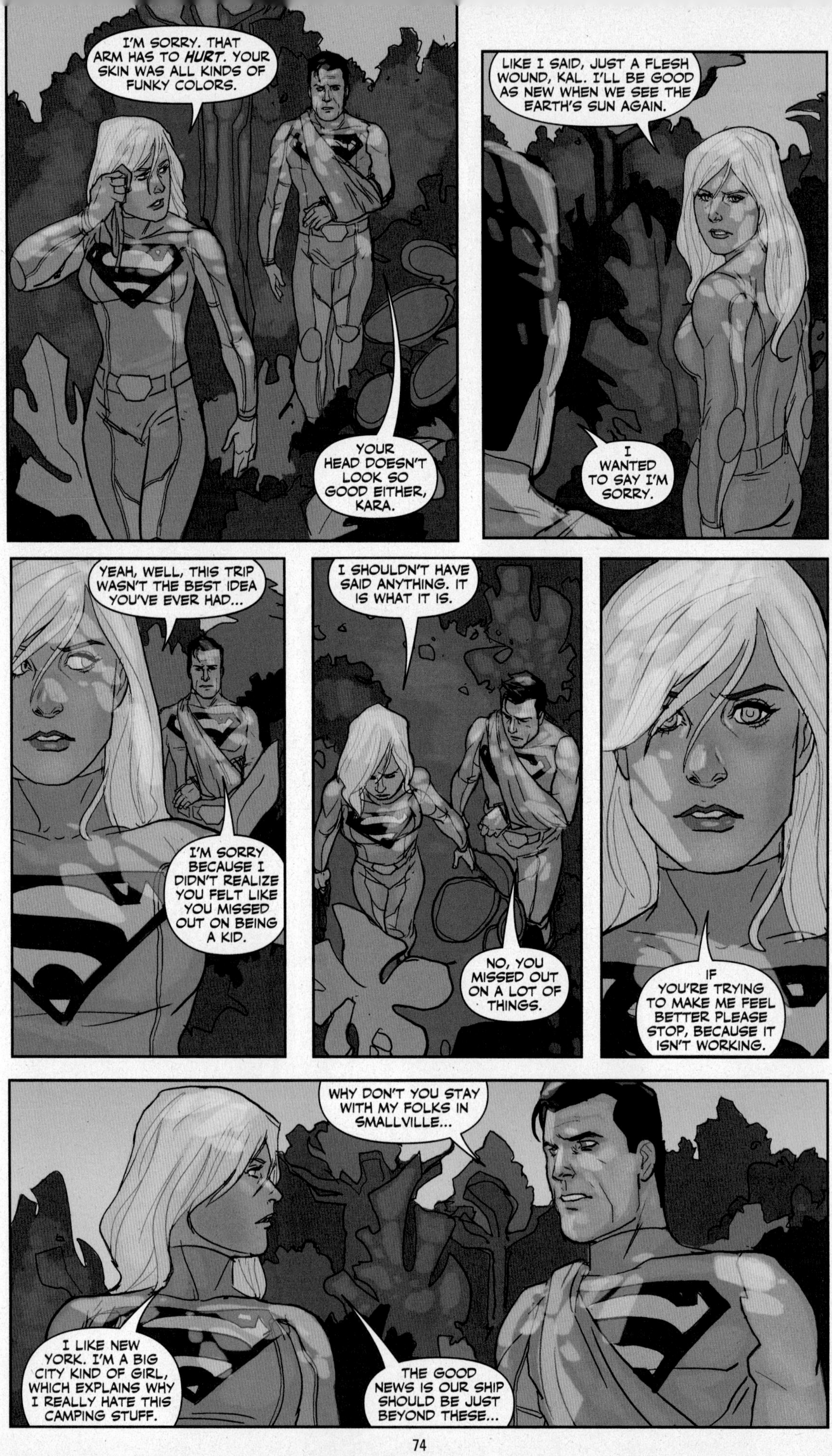
I'M SORRY. THAT ARM HAS TO *HURT*. YOUR SKIN WAS ALL KINDS OF FUNKY COLORS.
YOUR HEAD DOESN'T LOOK SO GOOD EITHER, KARA.
LIKE I SAID, JUST A FLESH WOUND, KAL. I'LL BE GOOD AS NEW WHEN WE SEE THE EARTH'S SUN AGAIN.
I WANTED TO SAY I'M SORRY.
YEAH, WELL, THIS TRIP WASN'T THE BEST IDEA YOU'VE EVER HAD...
I'M SORRY BECAUSE I DIDN'T REALIZE YOU FELT LIKE YOU MISSED OUT ON BEING A KID.
I SHOULDN'T HAVE SAID ANYTHING. IT IS WHAT IT IS.
NO, YOU MISSED OUT ON A LOT OF THINGS.
IF YOU'RE TRYING TO MAKE ME FEEL BETTER PLEASE STOP, BECAUSE IT ISN'T WORKING.
WHY DON'T YOU STAY WITH MY FOLKS IN SMALLVILLE...
I LIKE NEW YORK. I'M A BIG CITY KIND OF GIRL, WHICH EXPLAINS WHY I REALLY HATE THIS CAMPING STUFF.
THE GOOD NEWS IS OUR SHIP SHOULD BE JUST BEYOND THESE...

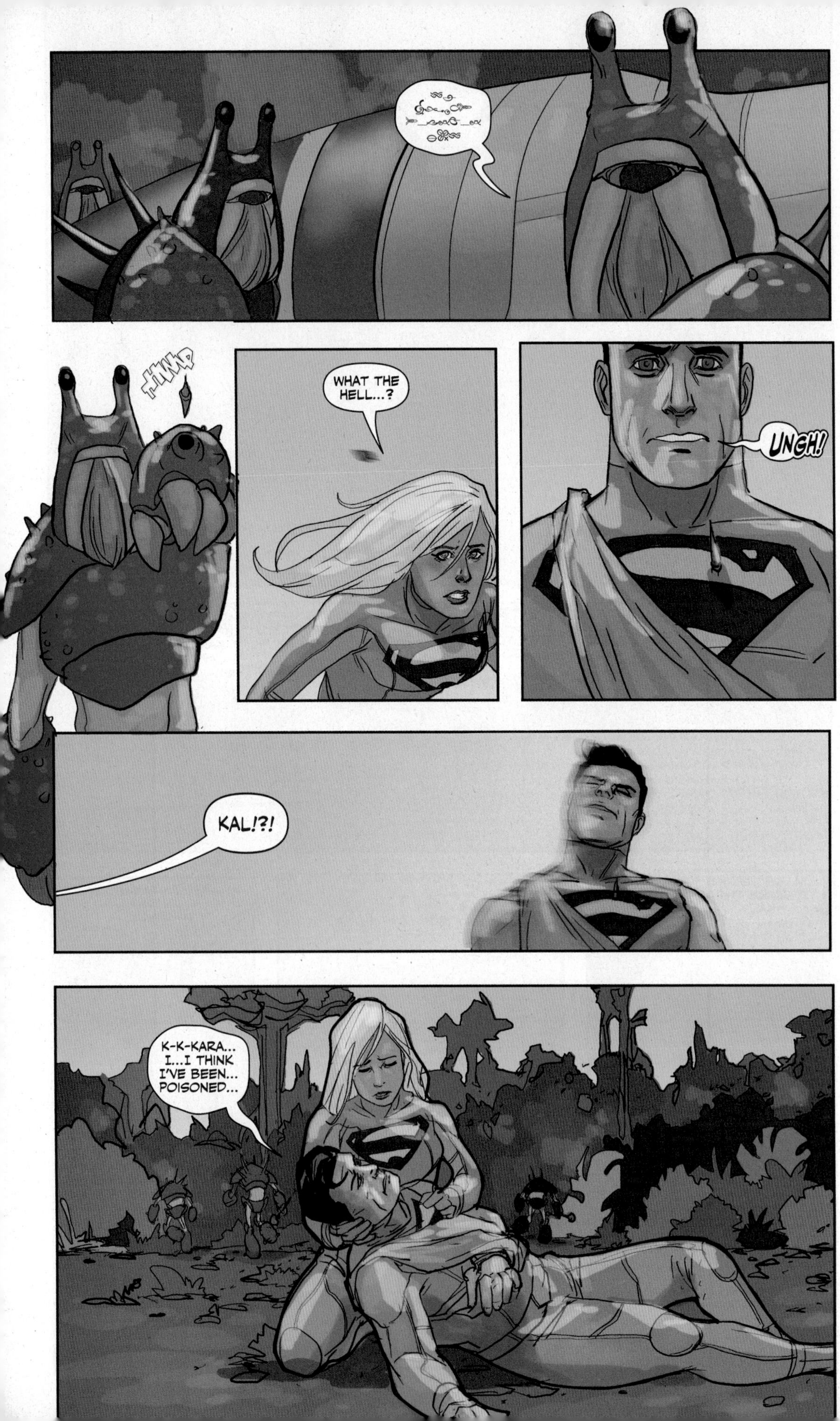
THWIP
WHAT THE HELL...?
UNGH!
KAL!?!
K-K-KARA...
I...I THINK
I'VE BEEN...
POISONED...

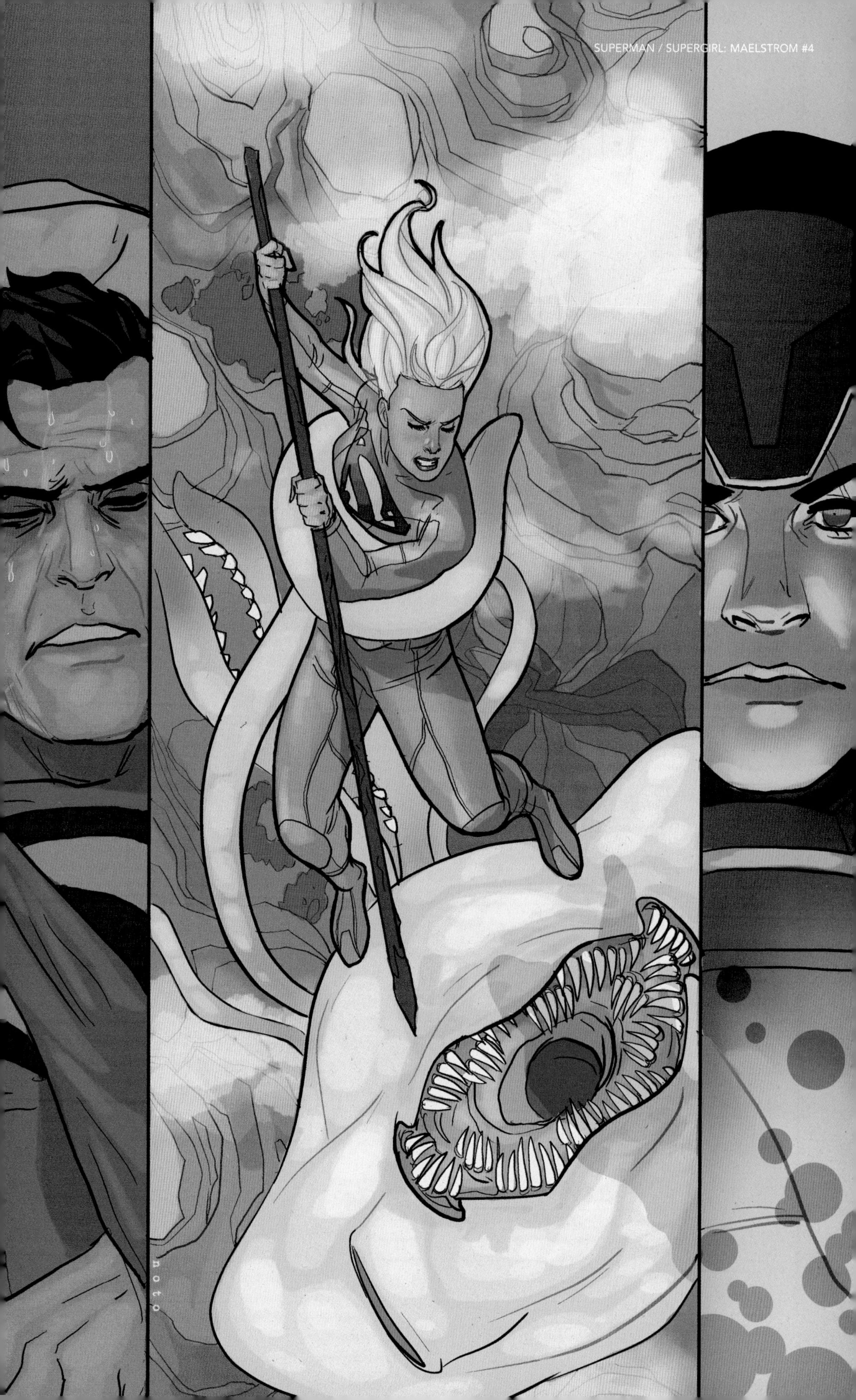
SUPERMAN / SUPERGIRL: MAELSTROM #4
noto

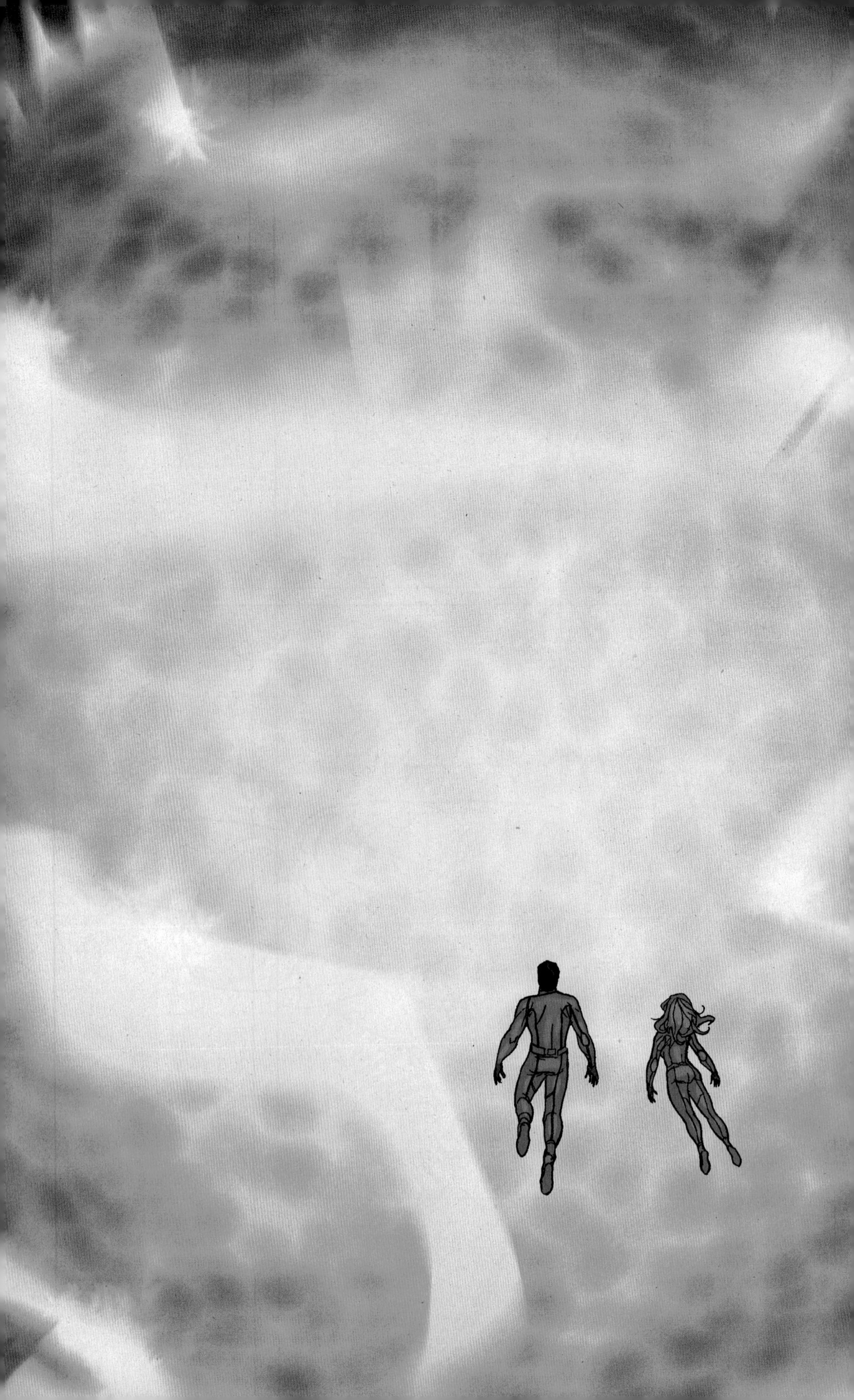

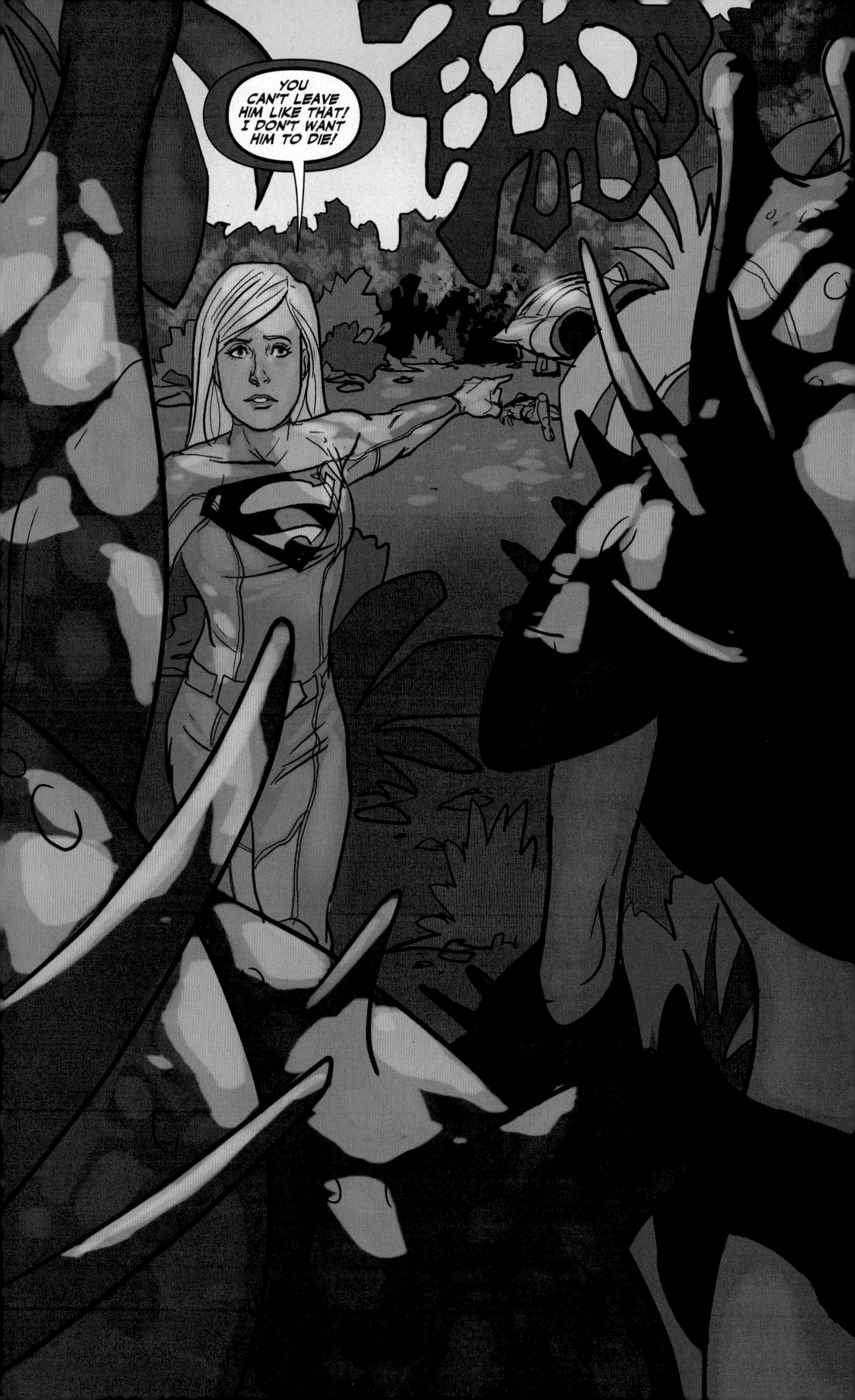
YOU CAN'T LEAVE HIM LIKE THAT! I DON'T WANT HIM TO DIE!

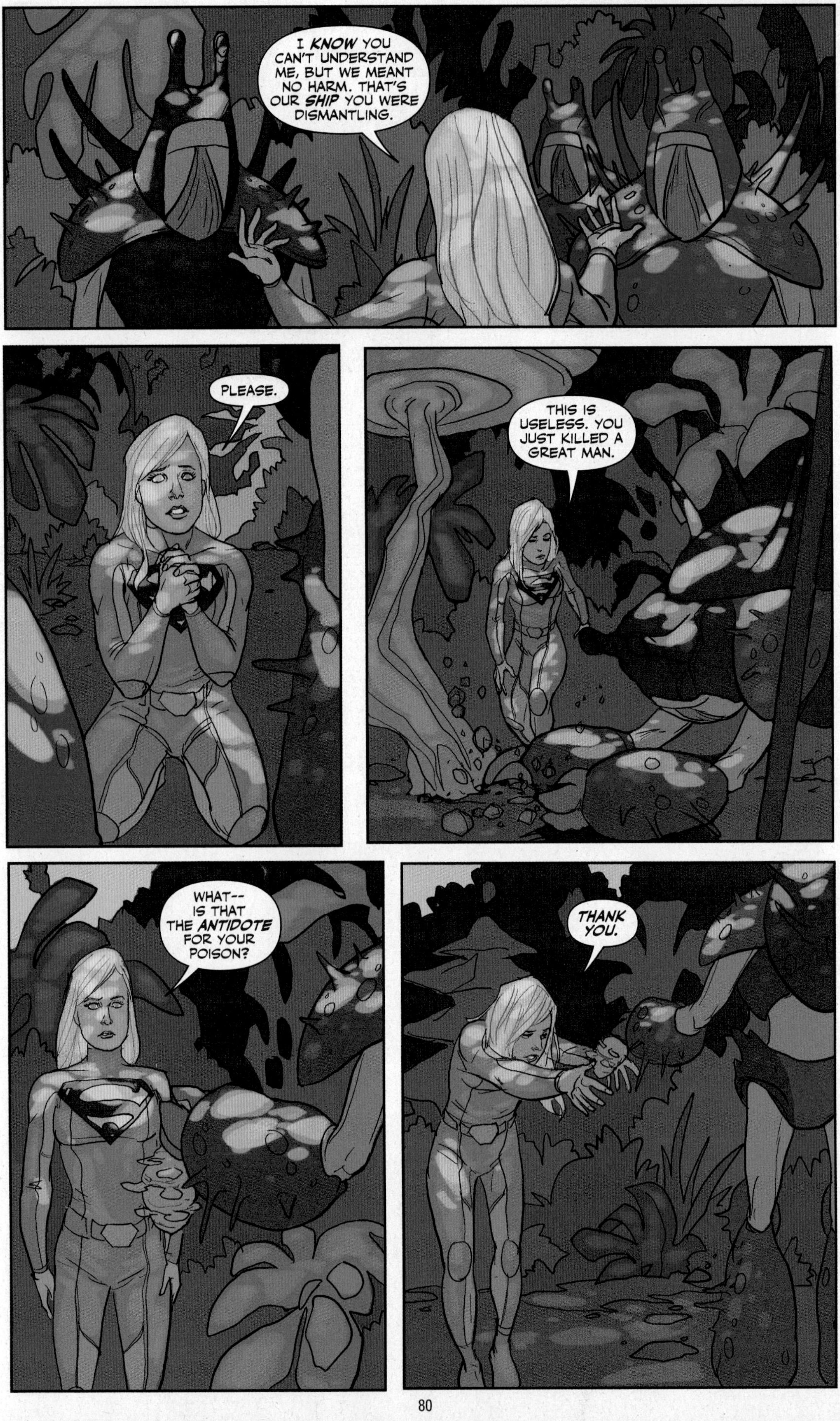
I KNOW YOU CAN'T UNDERSTAND ME, BUT WE MEANT NO HARM. THAT'S OUR SHIP YOU WERE DISMANTLING.
PLEASE.
THIS IS USELESS. YOU JUST KILLED A GREAT MAN.
WHAT-- IS THAT THE ANTIDOTE FOR YOUR POISON?
THANK YOU.

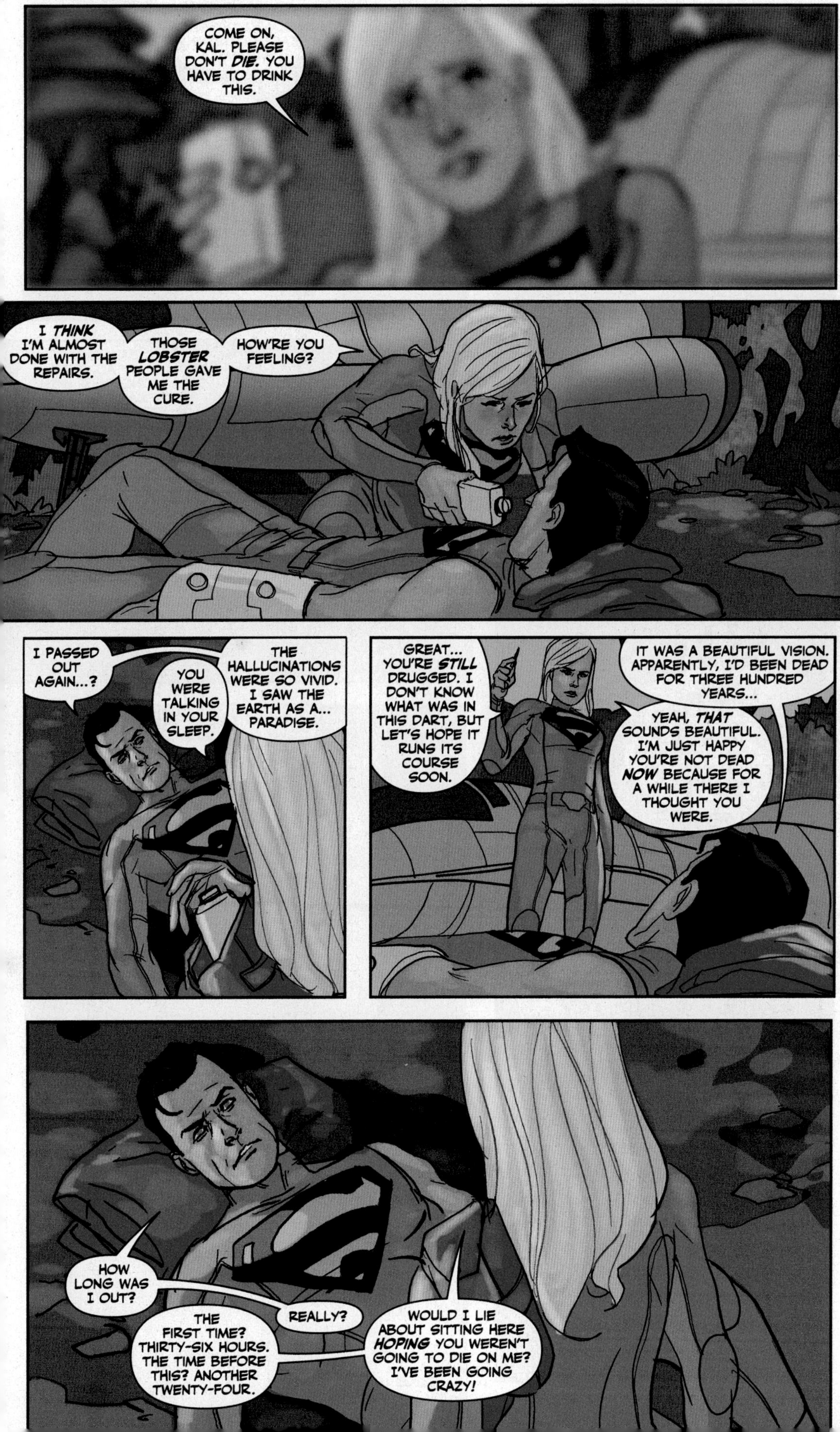
COME ON, KAL. PLEASE DON'T DIE. YOU HAVE TO DRINK THIS.
I THINK I'M ALMOST DONE WITH THE REPAIRS.
THOSE LOBSTER PEOPLE GAVE ME THE CURE.
HOW'RE YOU FEELING?
I PASSED OUT AGAIN...?
YOU WERE TALKING IN YOUR SLEEP.
THE HALLUCINATIONS WERE SO VIVID. I SAW THE EARTH AS A... PARADISE.
GREAT... YOU'RE STILL DRUGGED. I DON'T KNOW WHAT WAS IN THIS DART, BUT LET'S HOPE IT RUNS ITS COURSE SOON.
IT WAS A BEAUTIFUL VISION. APPARENTLY, I'D BEEN DEAD FOR THREE HUNDRED YEARS...
YEAH, THAT SOUNDS BEAUTIFUL. I'M JUST HAPPY YOU'RE NOT DEAD NOW BECAUSE FOR A WHILE THERE I THOUGHT YOU WERE.
HOW LONG WAS I OUT?
THE FIRST TIME? THIRTY-SIX HOURS. THE TIME BEFORE THIS? ANOTHER TWENTY-FOUR.
REALLY?
WOULD I LIE ABOUT SITTING HERE HOPING YOU WEREN'T GOING TO DIE ON ME? I'VE BEEN GOING CRAZY!

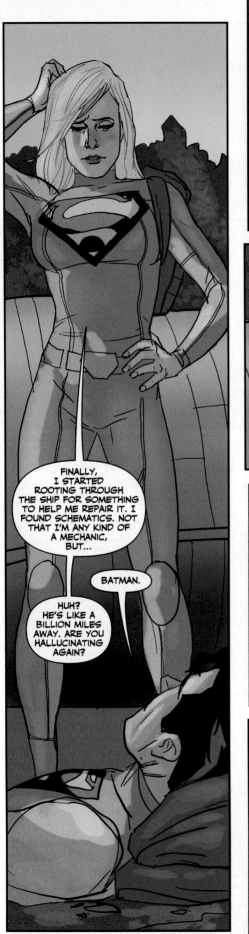

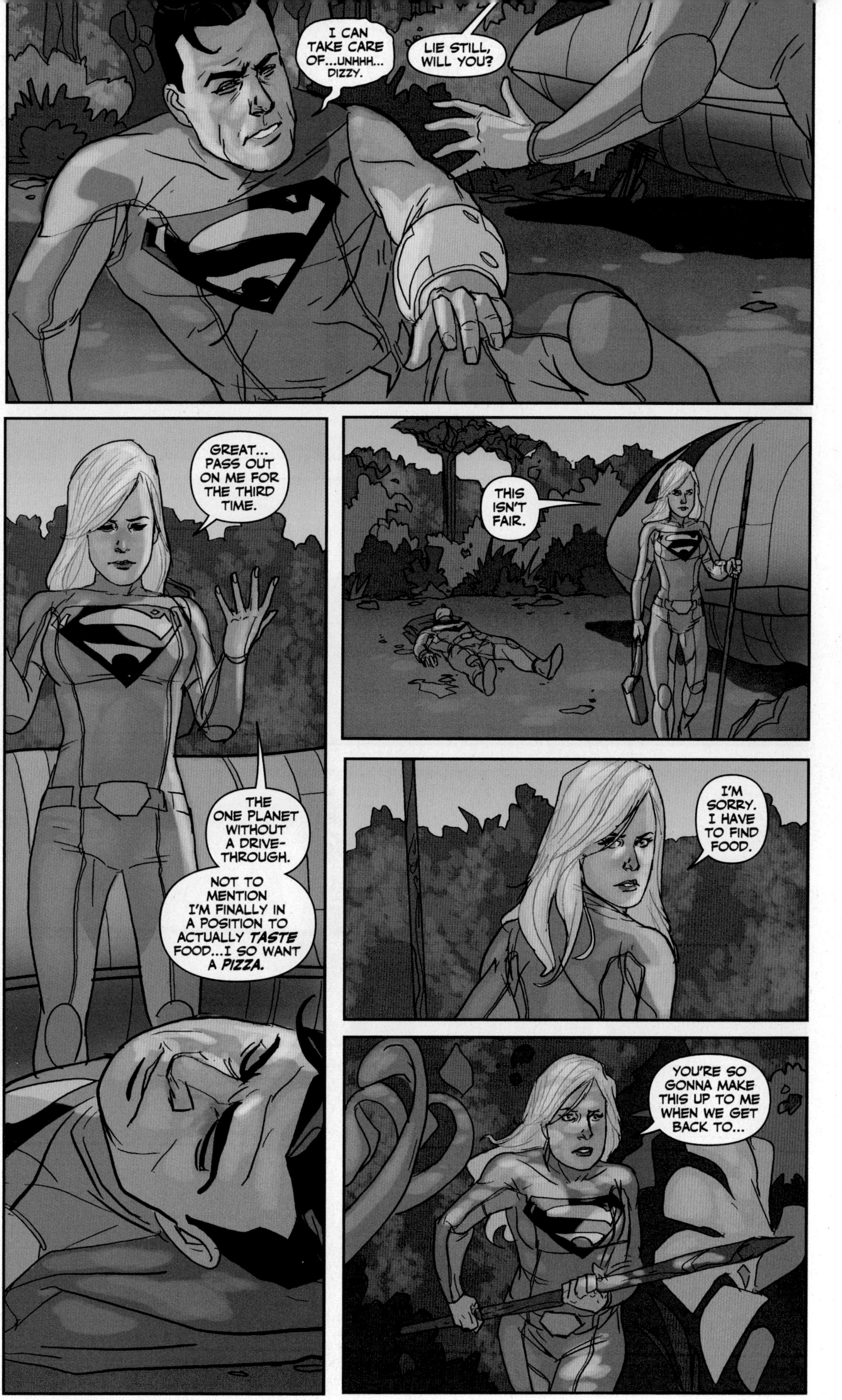
I CAN TAKE CARE OF...UNHHH... DIZZY.
LIE STILL, WILL YOU?
GREAT... PASS OUT ON ME FOR THE THIRD TIME.
THE ONE PLANET WITHOUT A DRIVE-THROUGH.
NOT TO MENTION I'M FINALLY IN A POSITION TO ACTUALLY *TASTE* FOOD...I SO WANT A *PIZZA.*
THIS ISN'T FAIR.
I'M SORRY. I HAVE TO FIND FOOD.
YOU'RE SO GONNA MAKE THIS UP TO ME WHEN WE GET BACK TO...

84

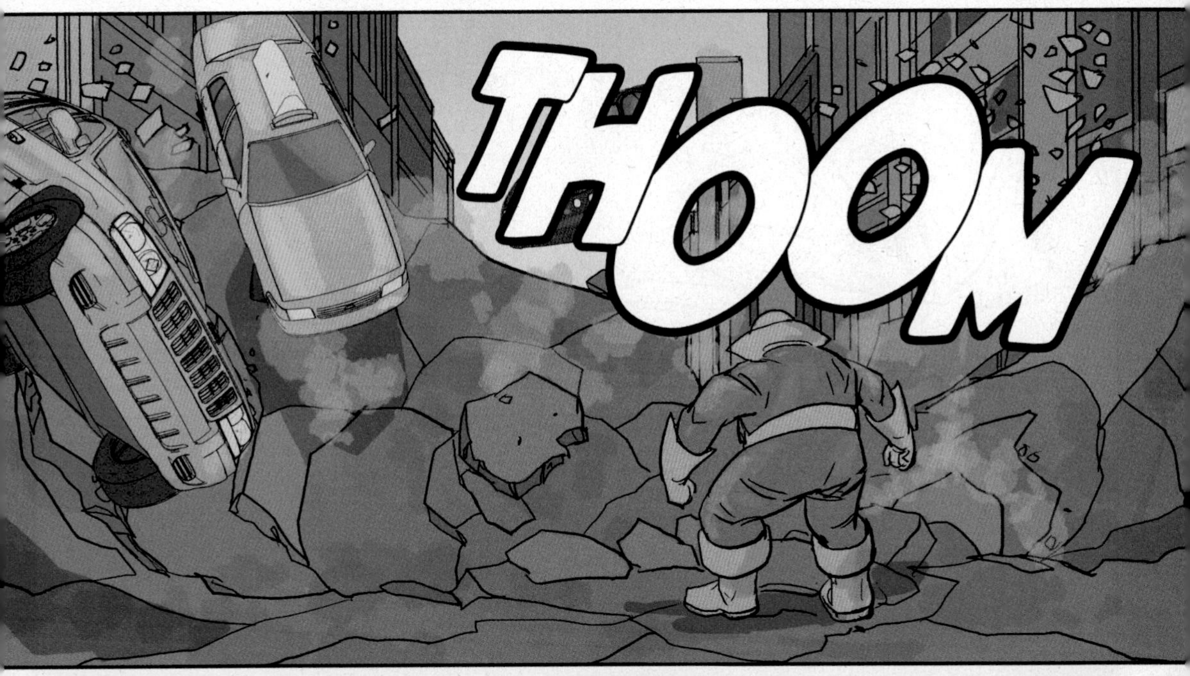
THOOM

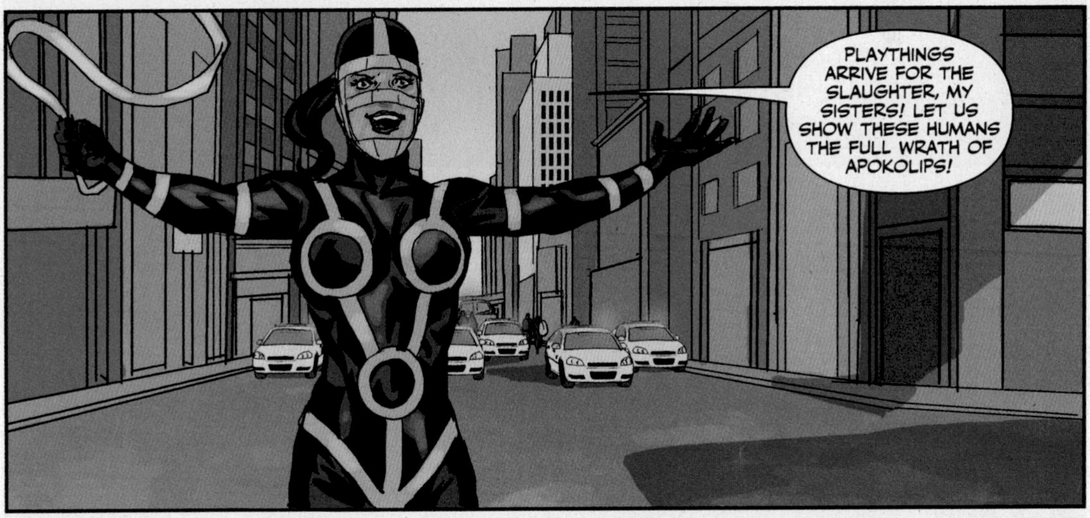
PLAYTHINGS ARRIVE FOR THE SLAUGHTER, MY SISTERS! LET US SHOW THESE HUMANS THE FULL WRATH OF APOKOLIPS!

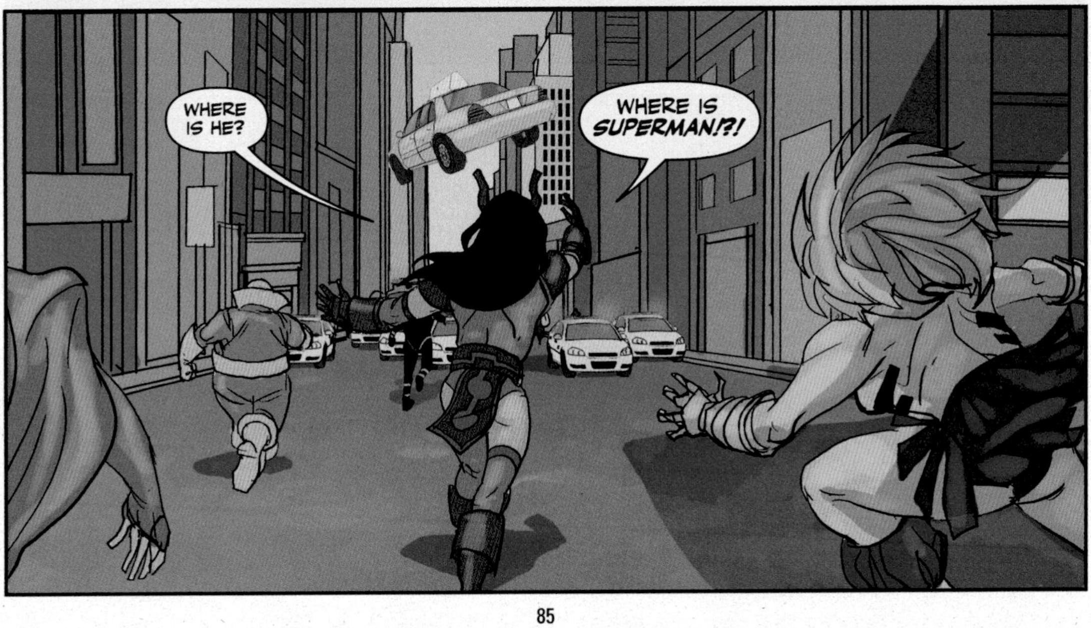
WHERE IS HE?
WHERE IS *SUPERMAN!?!*

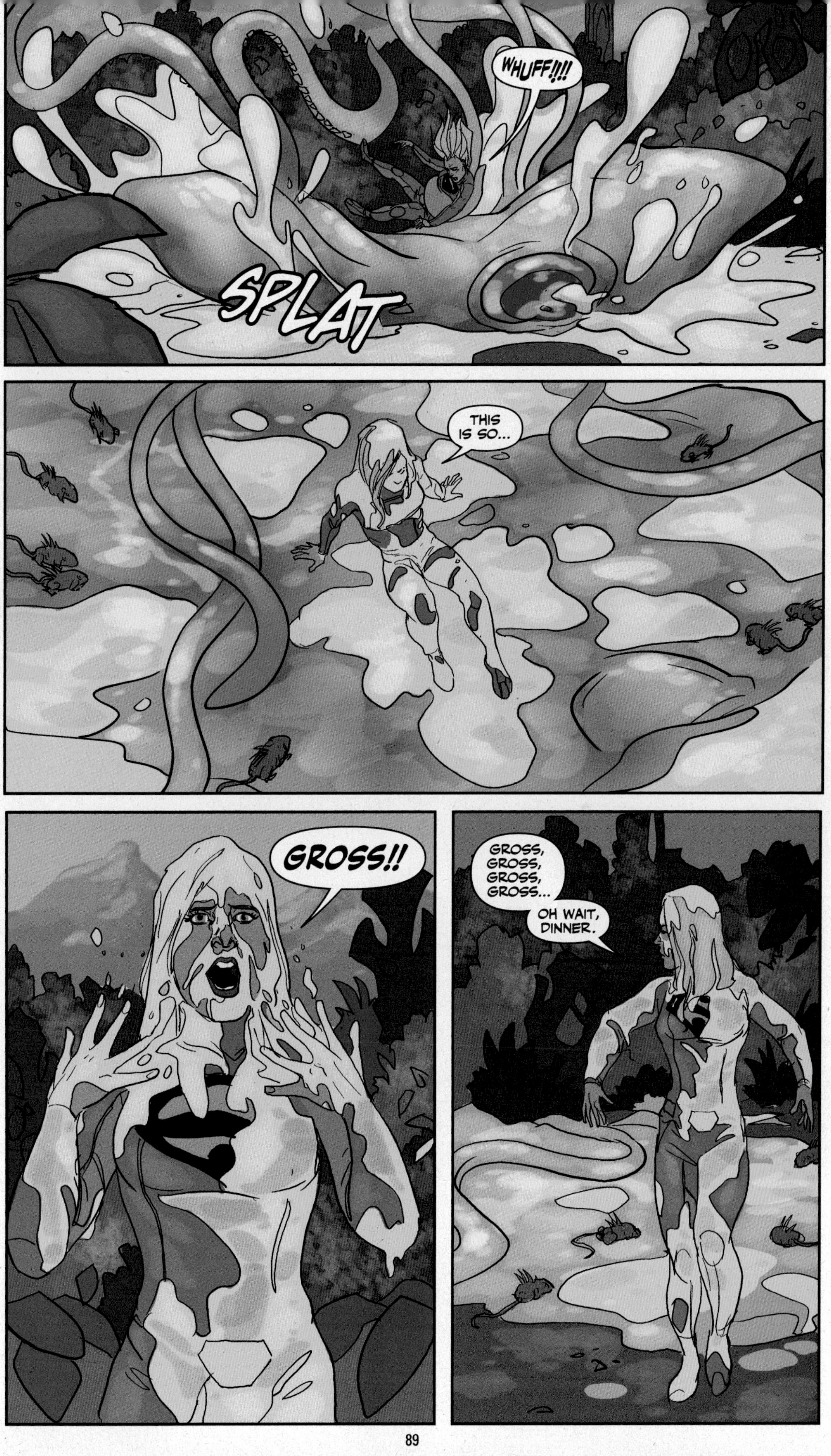
WHUFF!!!!
SPLAT
THIS IS SO...
GROSS!!
GROSS, GROSS, GROSS, GROSS...
OH WAIT, DINNER.

91

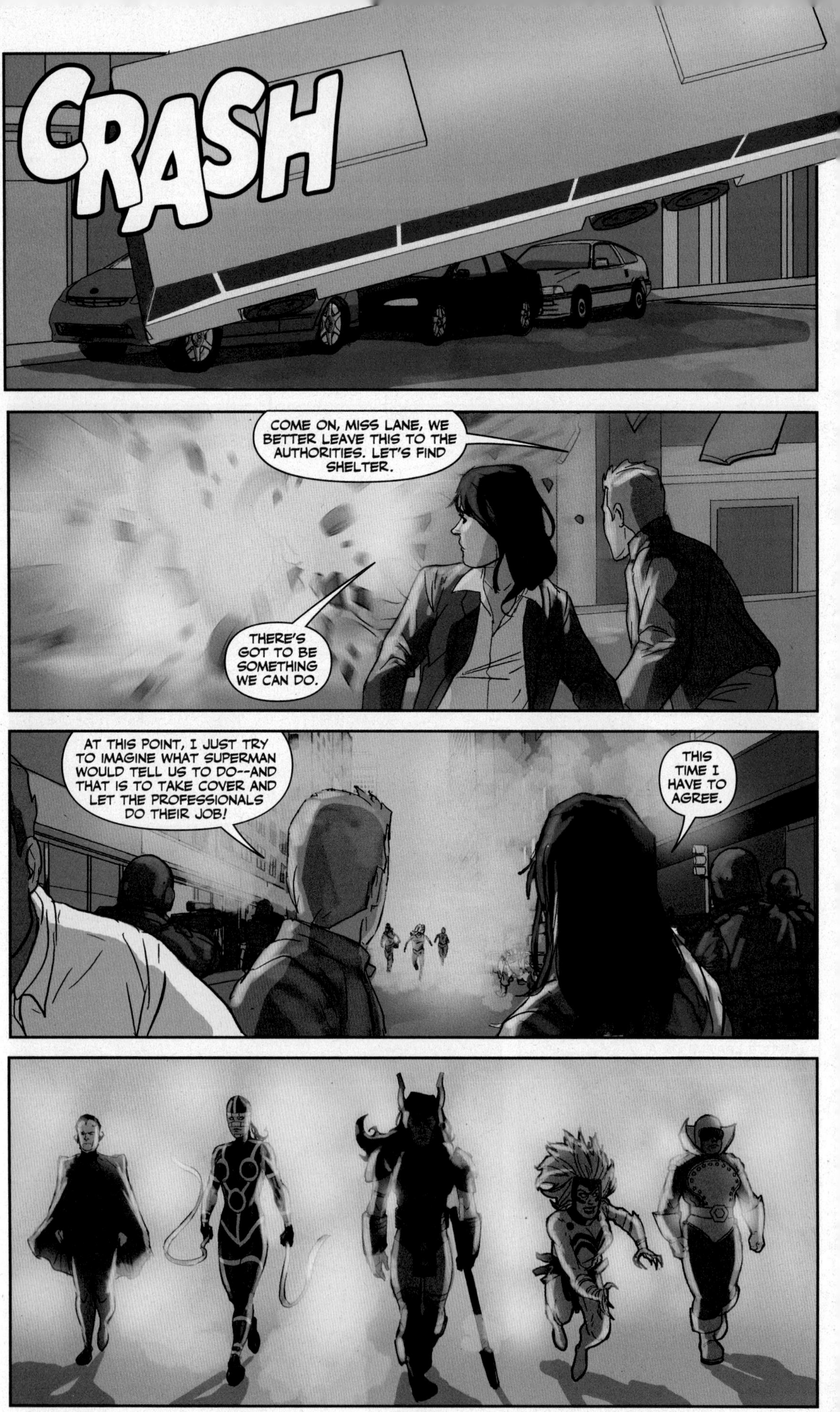
CRASH
COME ON, MISS LANE, WE BETTER LEAVE THIS TO THE AUTHORITIES. LET'S FIND SHELTER.
THERE'S GOT TO BE SOMETHING WE CAN DO.
AT THIS POINT, I JUST TRY TO IMAGINE WHAT SUPERMAN WOULD TELL US TO DO--AND THAT IS TO TAKE COVER AND LET THE PROFESSIONALS DO THEIR JOB!
THIS TIME I HAVE TO AGREE.

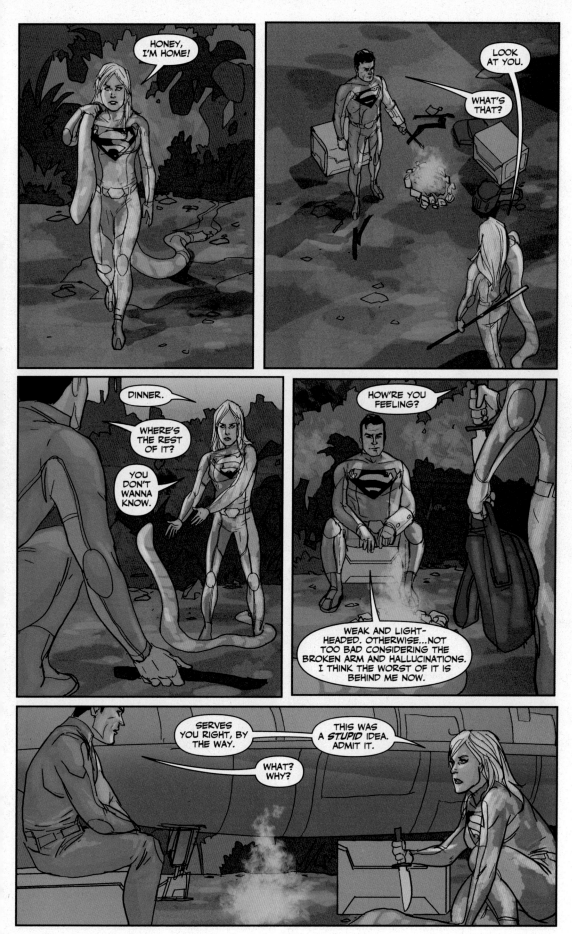

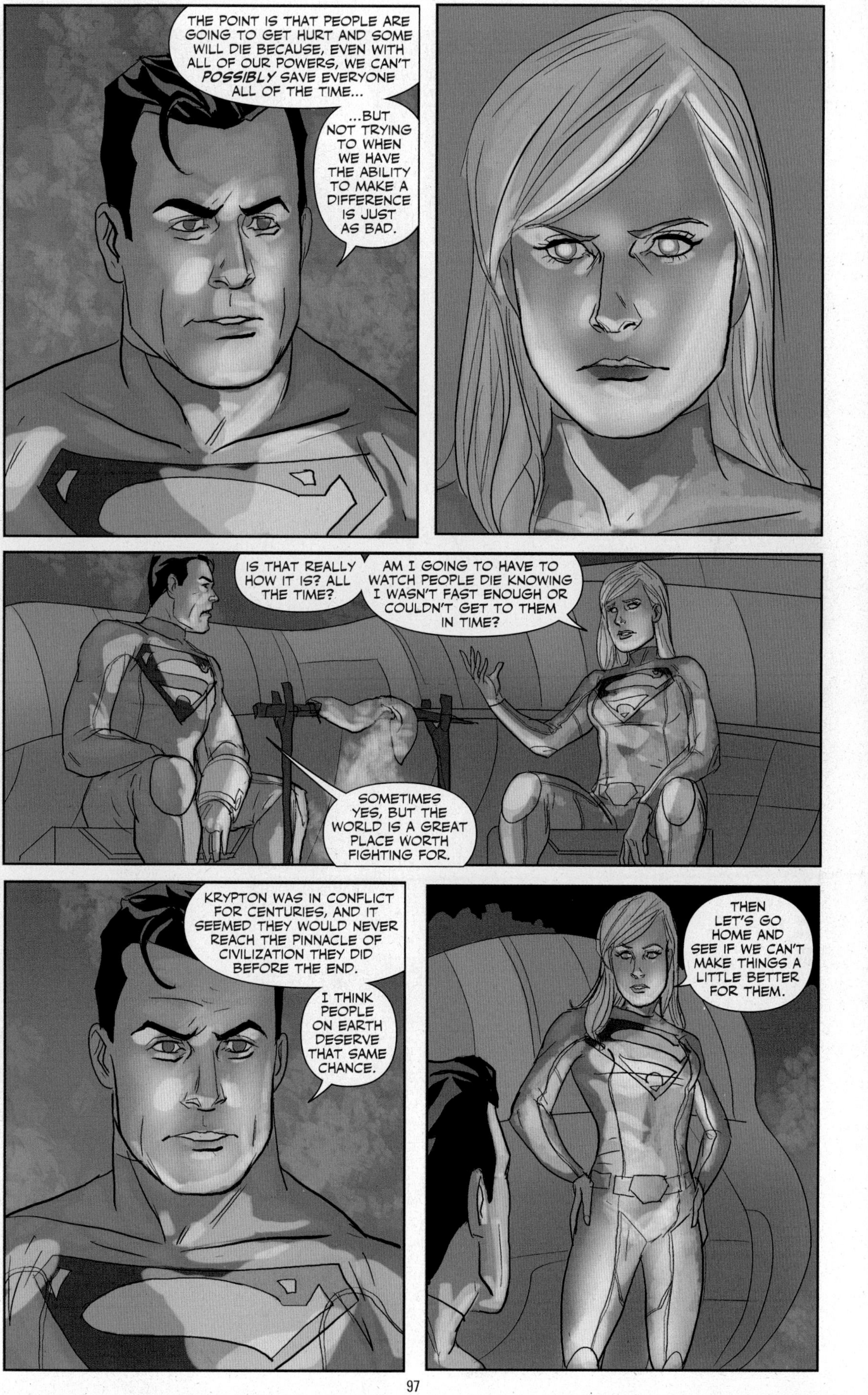
THE POINT IS THAT PEOPLE ARE GOING TO GET HURT AND SOME WILL DIE BECAUSE, EVEN WITH ALL OF OUR POWERS, WE CAN'T *POSSIBLY* SAVE EVERYONE ALL OF THE TIME...
...BUT NOT TRYING TO WHEN WE HAVE THE ABILITY TO MAKE A DIFFERENCE IS JUST AS BAD.
IS THAT REALLY HOW IT IS? ALL THE TIME?
AM I GOING TO HAVE TO WATCH PEOPLE DIE KNOWING I WASN'T FAST ENOUGH OR COULDN'T GET TO THEM IN TIME?
SOMETIMES YES, BUT THE WORLD IS A GREAT PLACE WORTH FIGHTING FOR.
KRYPTON WAS IN CONFLICT FOR CENTURIES, AND IT SEEMED THEY WOULD NEVER REACH THE PINNACLE OF CIVILIZATION THEY DID BEFORE THE END.
I THINK PEOPLE ON EARTH DESERVE THAT SAME CHANCE.
THEN LET'S GO HOME AND SEE IF WE CAN'T MAKE THINGS A LITTLE BETTER FOR THEM.

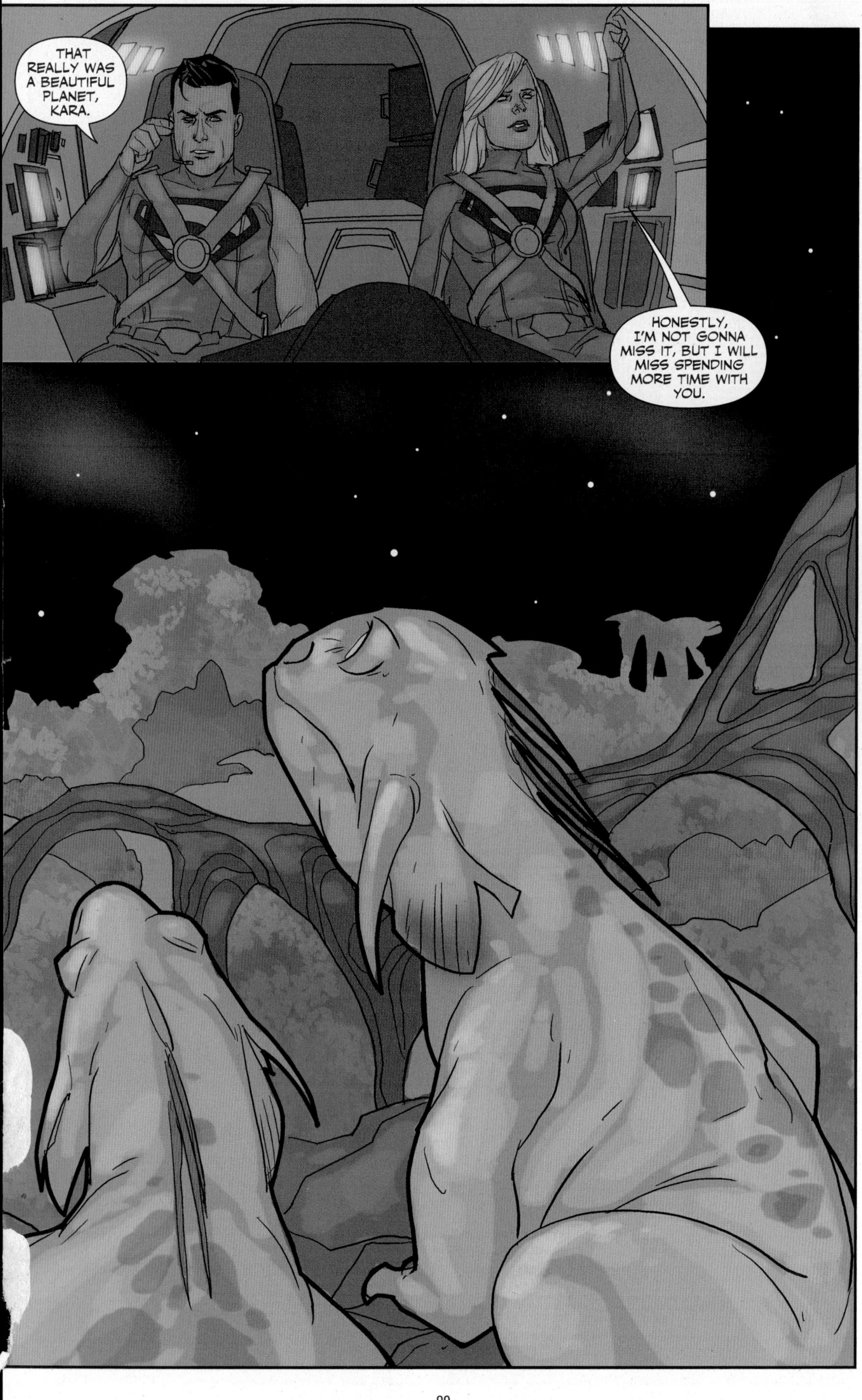
THAT REALLY WAS A BEAUTIFUL PLANET, KARA.
HONESTLY, I'M NOT GONNA MISS IT, BUT I WILL MISS SPENDING MORE TIME WITH YOU.

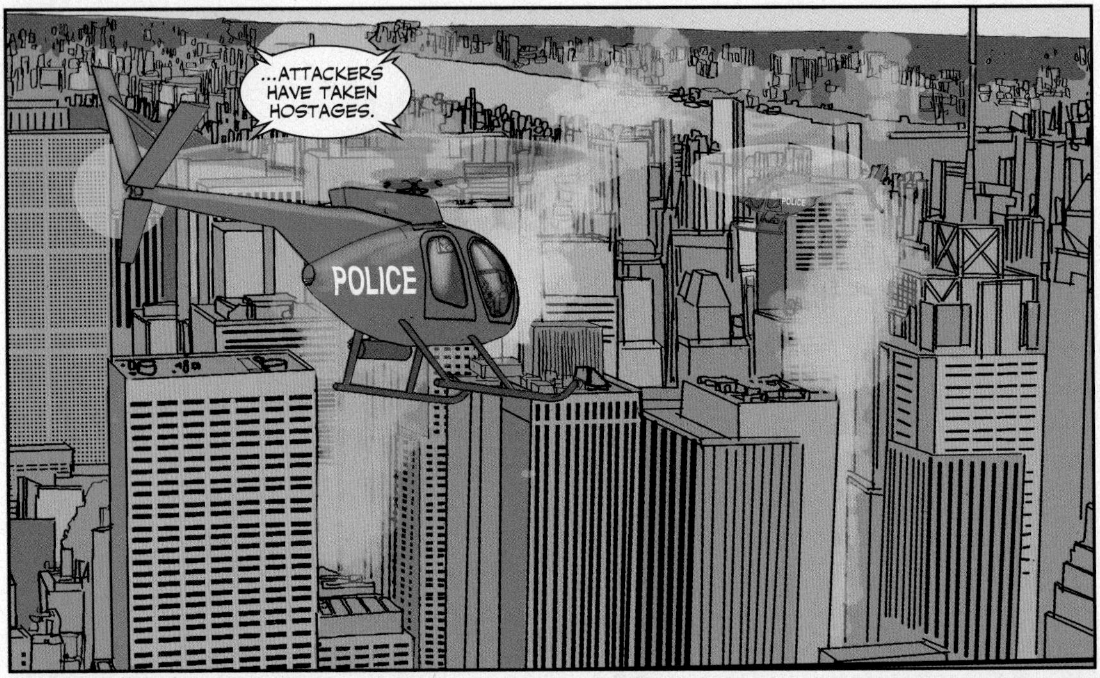
...ATTACKERS HAVE TAKEN HOSTAGES.
POLICE
POLICE

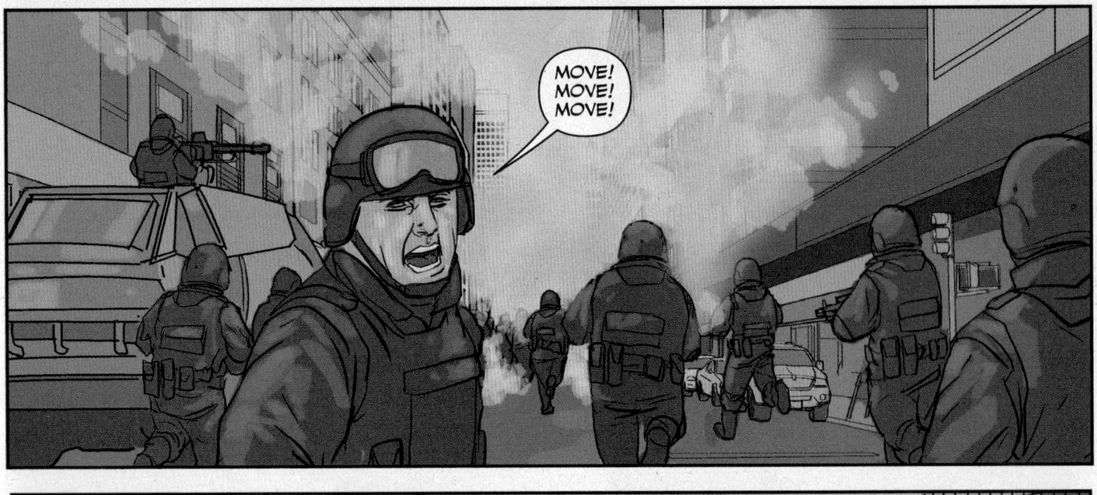
MOVE! MOVE! MOVE!

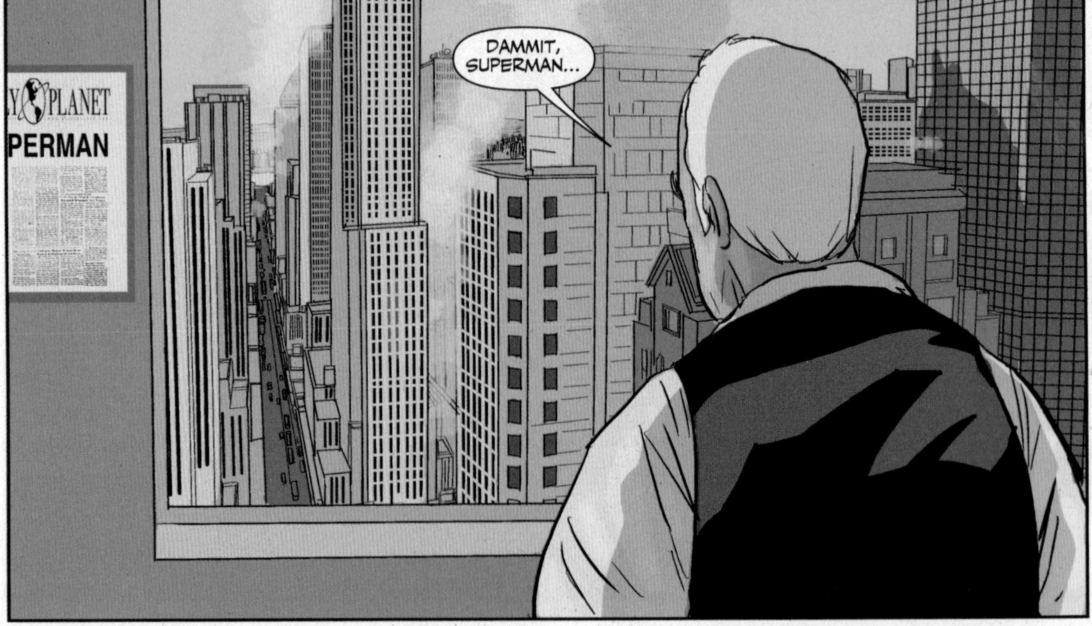
PLANET
PERMAN
DAMMIT, SUPERMAN...

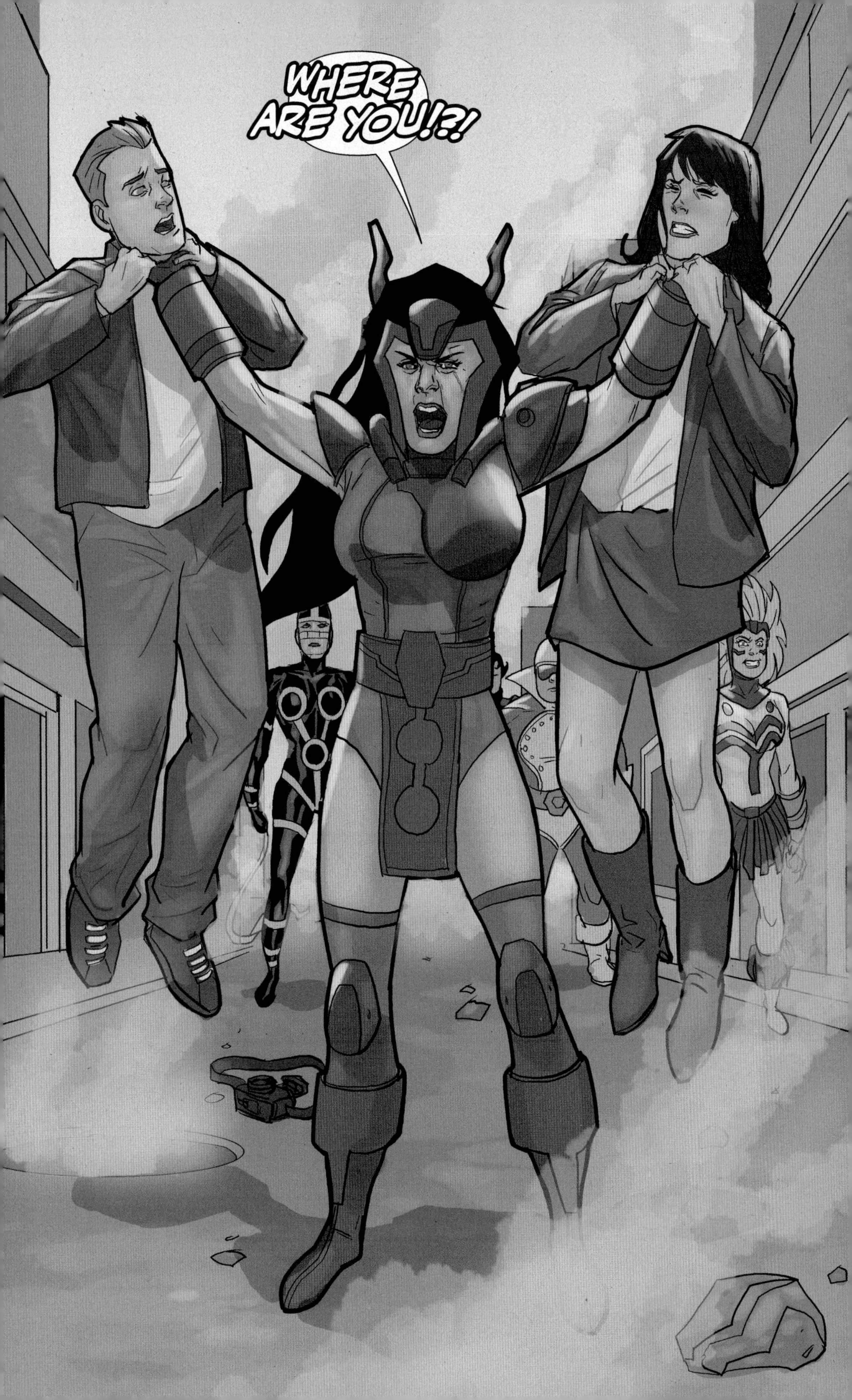
WHERE ARE YOU!?!

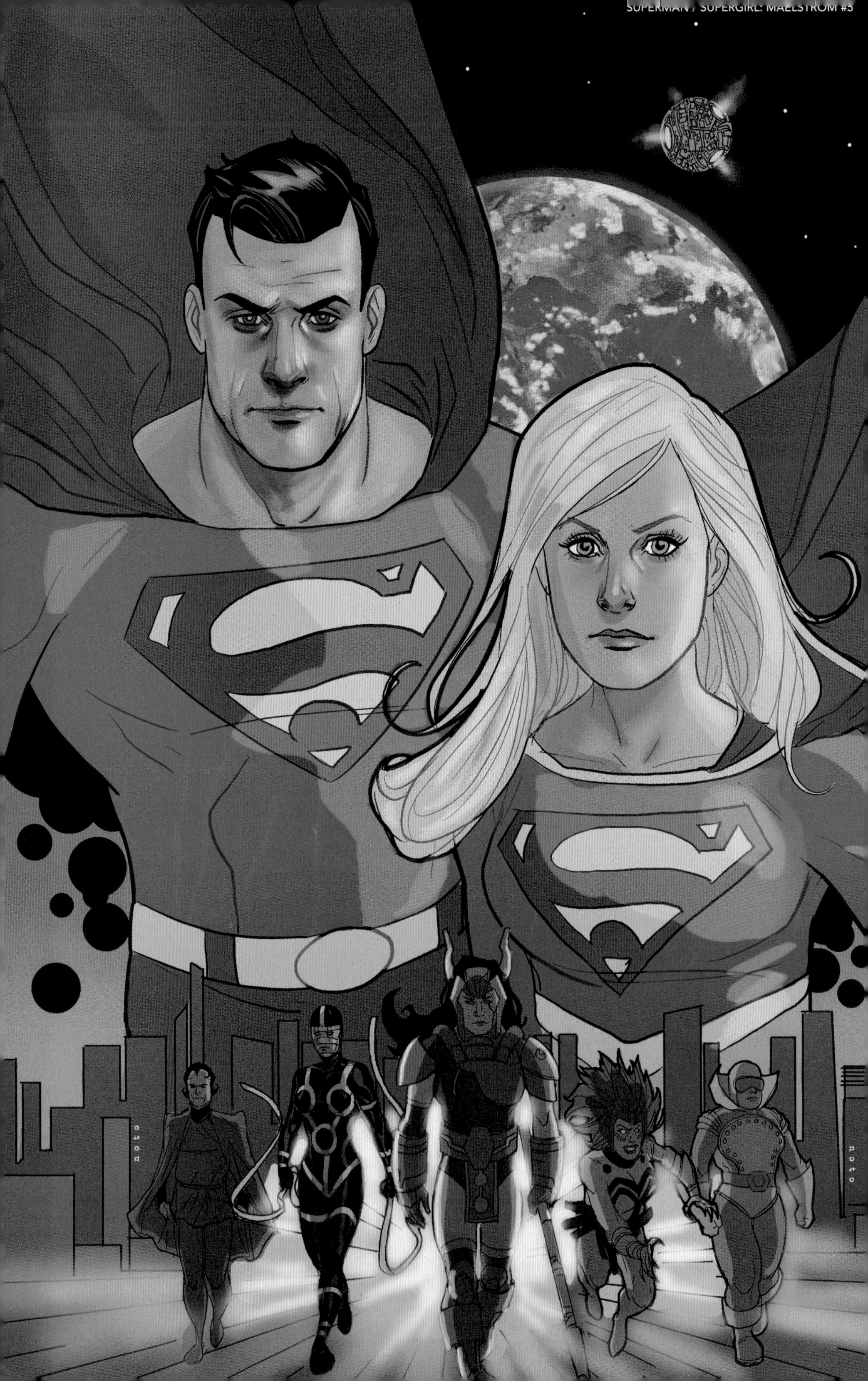
noto
noto

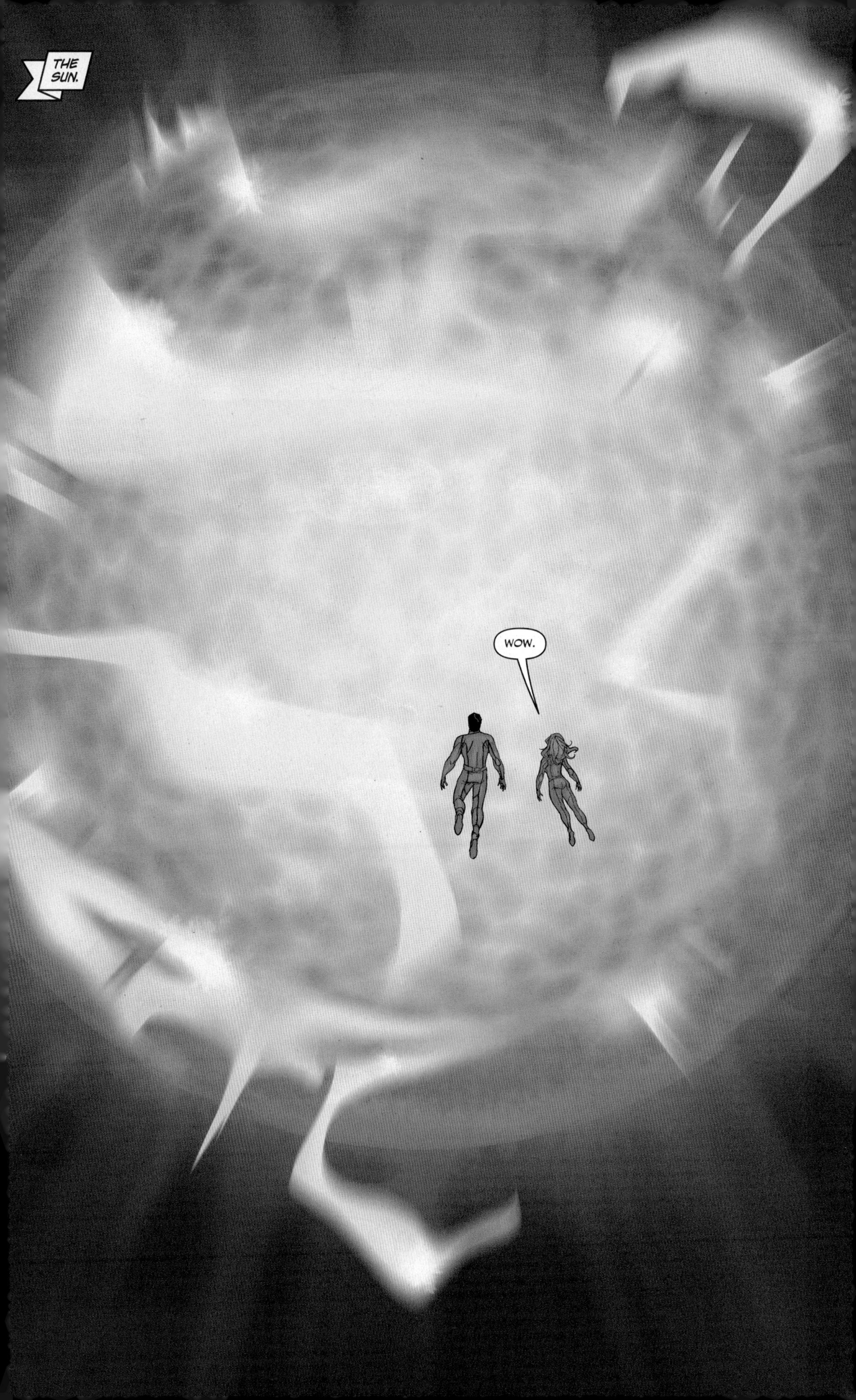
THE SUN.
WOW.

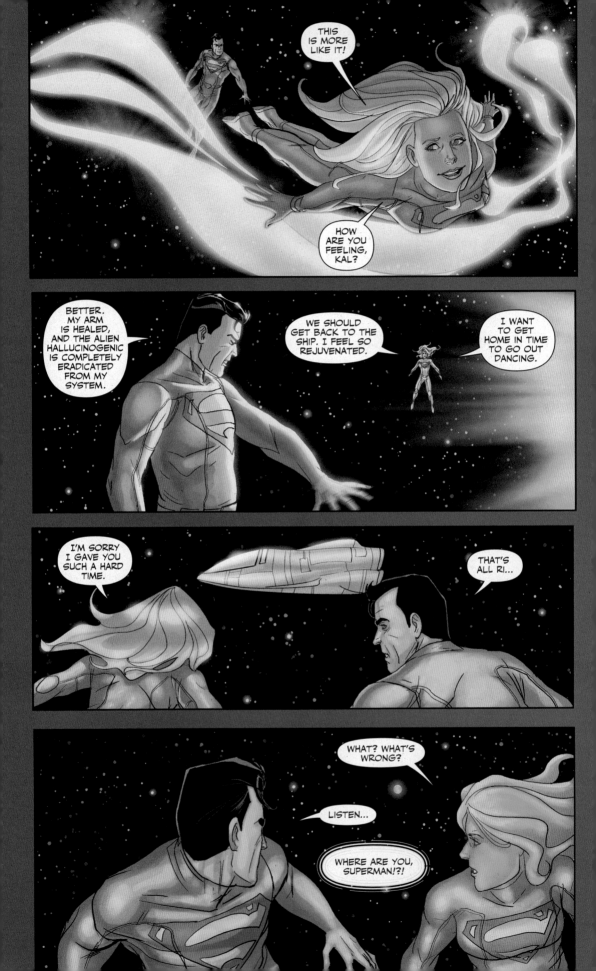

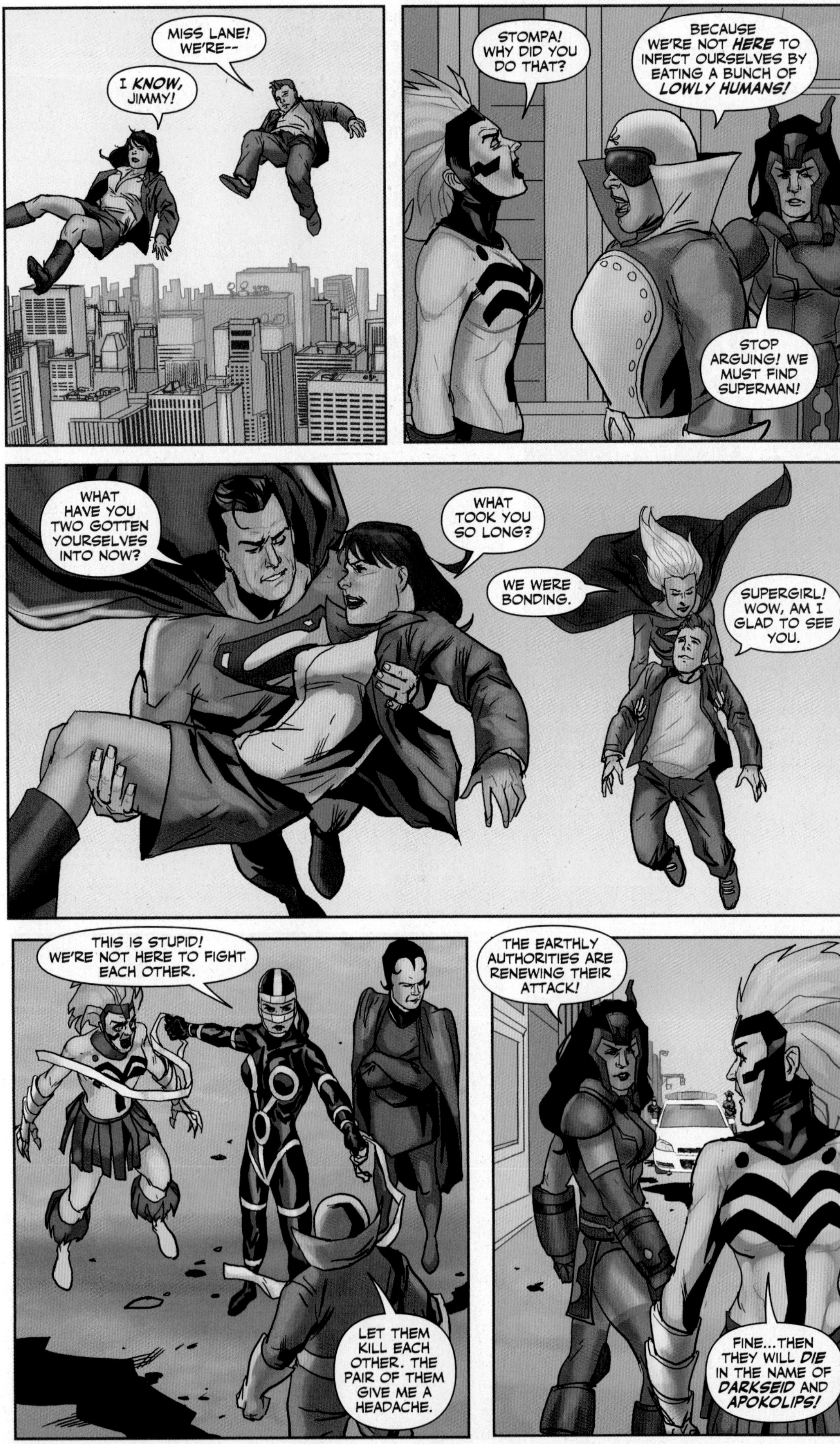
MISS LANE! WE'RE--
I KNOW, JIMMY!
STOMPA! WHY DID YOU DO THAT?
BECAUSE WE'RE NOT HERE TO INFECT OURSELVES BY EATING A BUNCH OF LOWLY HUMANS!
STOP ARGUING! WE MUST FIND SUPERMAN!
WHAT HAVE YOU TWO GOTTEN YOURSELVES INTO NOW?
WHAT TOOK YOU SO LONG?
WE WERE BONDING.
SUPERGIRL! WOW, AM I GLAD TO SEE YOU.
THIS IS STUPID! WE'RE NOT HERE TO FIGHT EACH OTHER.
LET THEM KILL EACH OTHER. THE PAIR OF THEM GIVE ME A HEADACHE.
THE EARTHLY AUTHORITIES ARE RENEWING THEIR ATTACK!
FINE...THEN THEY WILL DIE IN THE NAME OF DARKSEID AND APOKOLIPS!

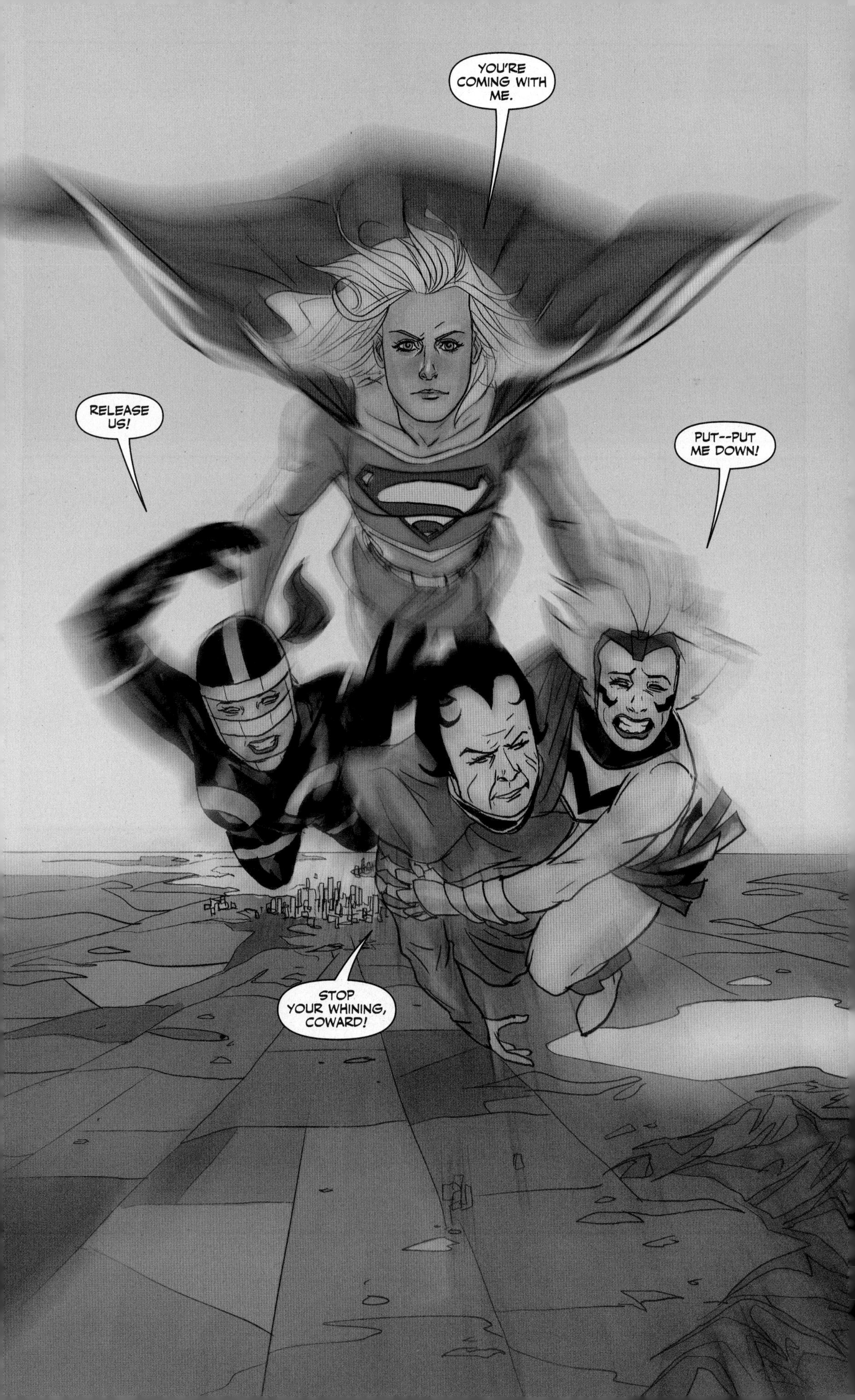
YOU'RE COMING WITH ME.
RELEASE US!
PUT--PUT ME DOWN!
STOP YOUR WHINING, COWARD!

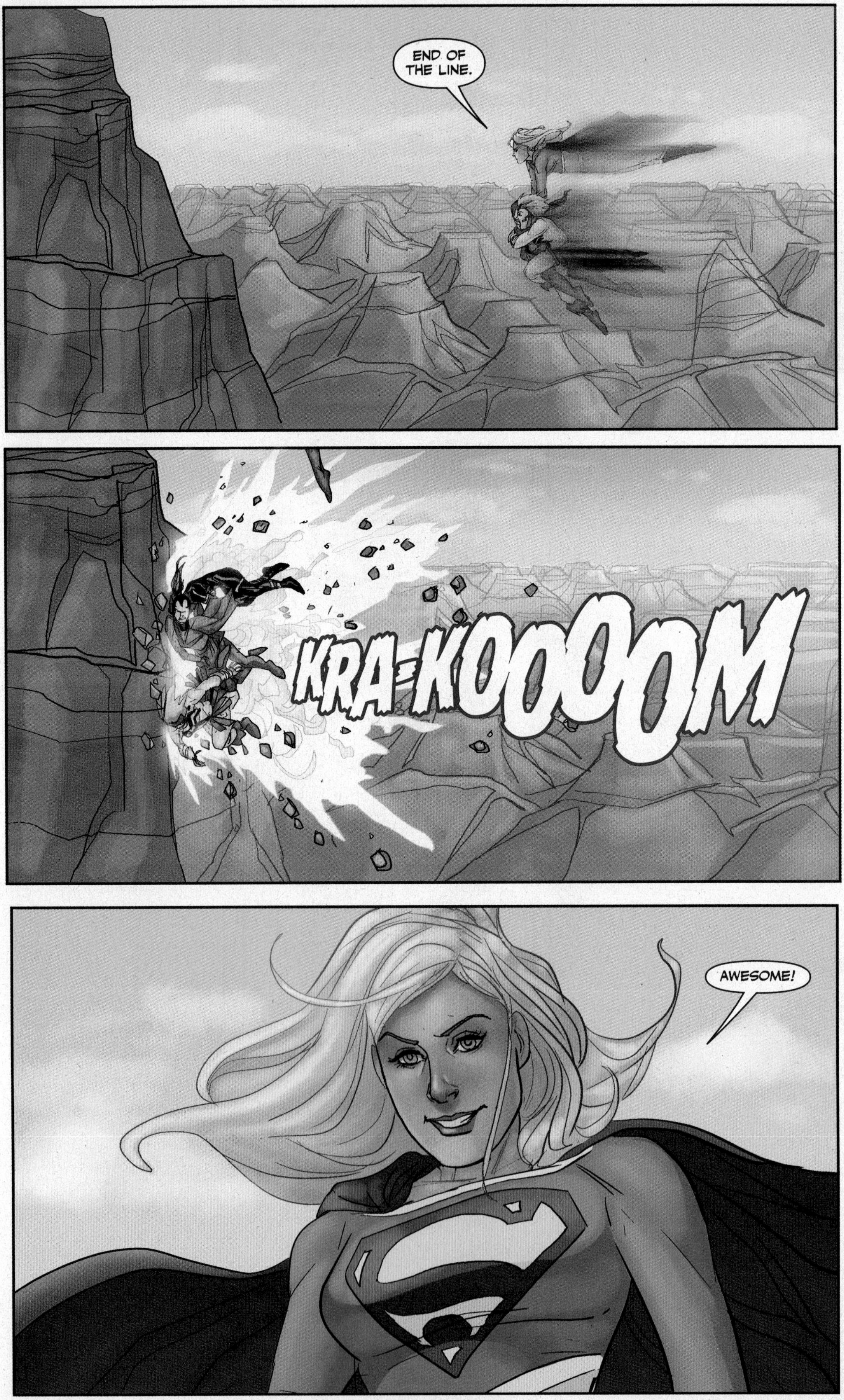
END OF THE LINE.
KRA-KOOOOOM
AWESOME!

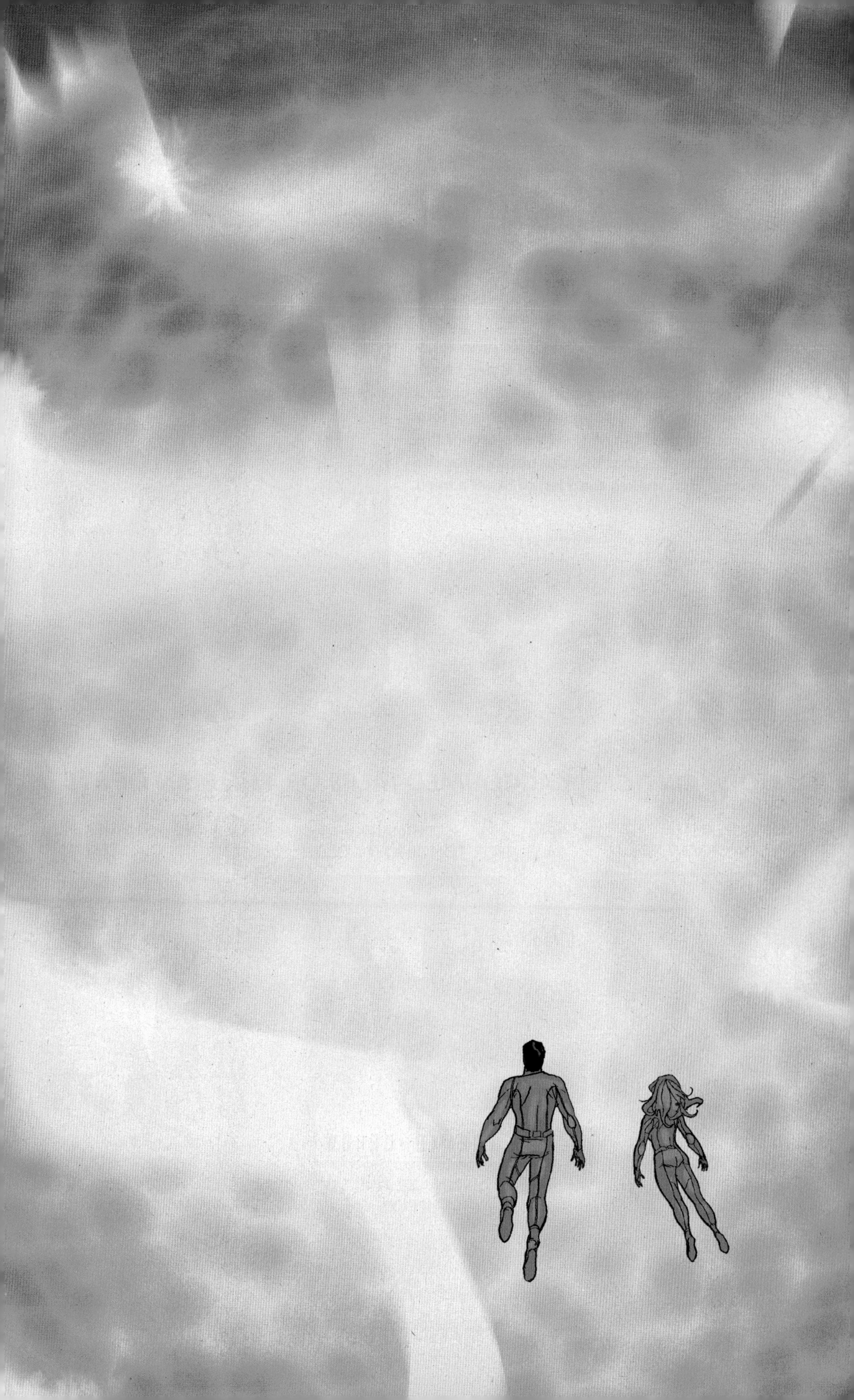

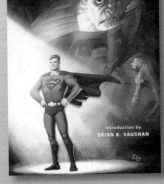

MORE CLASSIC TALES OF THE MAN OF STEEL

SUPERMAN:
THE MAN OF STEEL
VOLS. 1 - 6

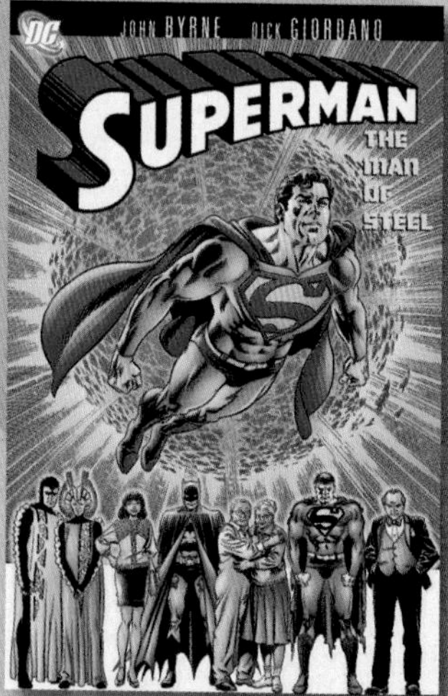
JOHN BYRNE
DICK GIORDANO
SUPERMAN
THE MAN OF STEEL

JOHN BYRNE

SUPERMAN:
BIRTHRIGHT

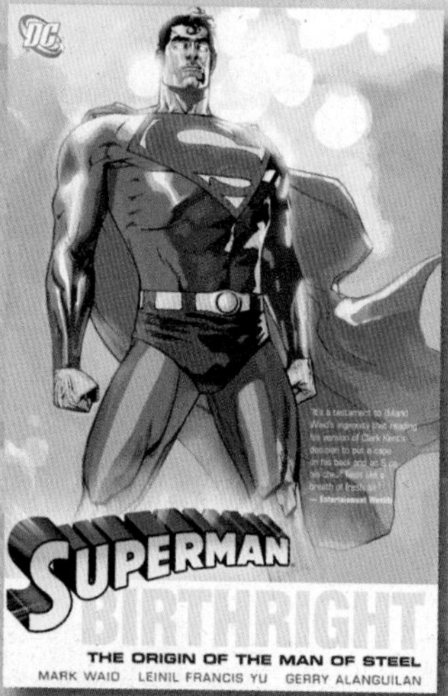
SUPERMAN
BIRTHRIGHT
THE ORIGIN OF THE MAN OF STEEL
MARK WAID LEINIL FRANCIS YU GERRY ALANGUILAN

MARK WAID
LEINIL YU

SUPERMAN:
CAMELOT FALLS
VOLS. 1 - 2

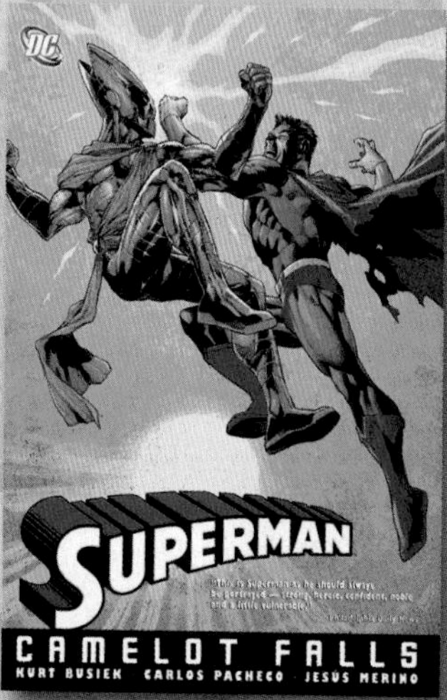
SUPERMAN
CAMELOT FALLS
KURT BUSIEK CARLOS PACHECO JESUS MERINO

KURT BUSIEK
CARLOS PACHECO

SUPERMAN:
OUR WORLDS AT WAR

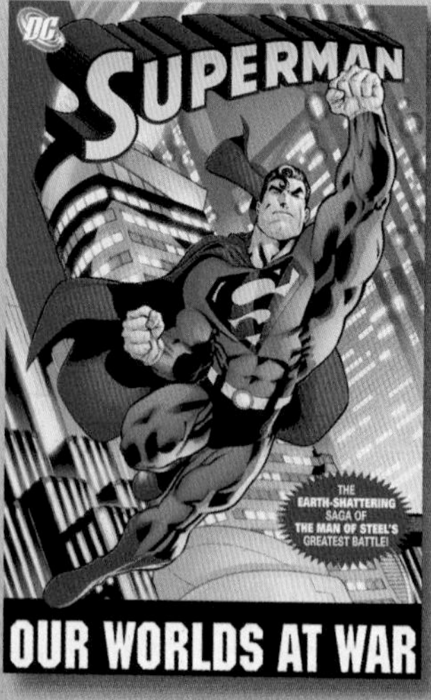
SUPERMAN
THE EARTH-SHATTERING SAGA OF THE MAN OF STEEL'S GREATEST BATTLE!
OUR WORLDS AT WAR

VARIOUS
WRITERS & ARTISTS

SUPERMAN:
RED SON

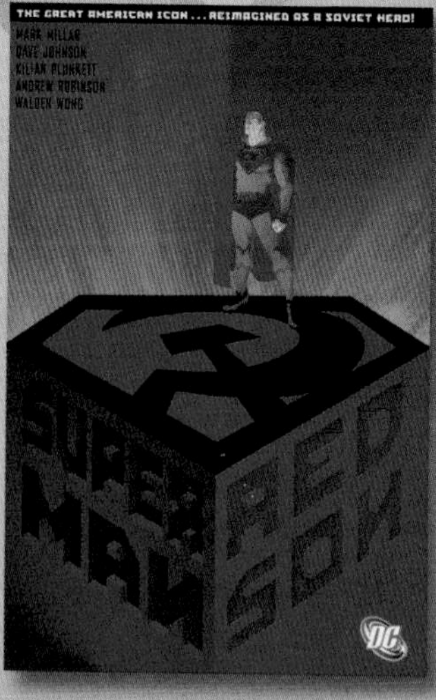
THE GREAT AMERICAN ICON... REIMAGINED AS A SOVIET HERO!

MARK MILLAR
DAVE JOHNSON
KILLIAN PLUNKETT

SUPERMAN:
SECRET IDENTITY

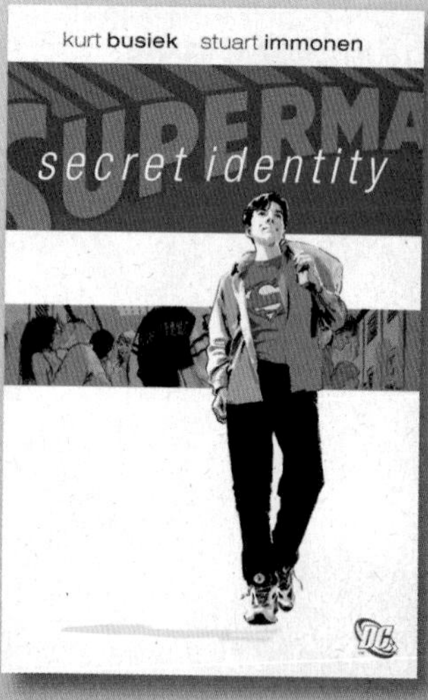
kurt busiek stuart immonen
secret identity

KURT BUSIEK
STUART IMMONEN

SEARCH THE GRAPHIC NOVELS SECTION OF
DCCOMICS.COM
FOR ART AND INFORMATION ON ALL OF OUR BOOKS!